JASPER
KIM

AMERICAN LAW 101

AN EASY PRIMER ON THE U.S. LEGAL SYSTEM

Cover design by Kelly Book/ABA publishing.

Printed in the United States of America.

27 26 25 24 5 4

Library of Congress Cataloging-in-Publication Data

Kim, Jasper, author.
American law 101: an easy primer on the U.S. legal system / by Jasper Kim.
pages cm.
Includes bibliographical references and index.
ISBN 978-1-62722-858-9 (alk. paper)
1. Law—United States. 2. Jurisprudence—United States. 3. Justice, Administration of—United States. I. Title. II. Title: American law one hundred one. III. Title: American law one hundred and one.
KF385.K56 2014
349.73—dc23

2014041055

This book is dedicated to my family, my friends, and the countless people who shaped and influenced my life.

TABLE OF CONTENTS

INTRODUCTION

American Law 101: An Easy Primer on the U.S. Legal System is a simple and reader-friendly primer on American law principles geared for a wide audience of both lawyers and non-lawyers worldwide.

American Law 101 covers both the spirit and "black letter law" principles underlying the American legal system. In terms of readership, *American Law 101* is geared towards an extremely broad spectrum, including American and foreign lawyers, business professionals, law and business students, and administrators, as well as the simply curious. *American Law 101* reaches its broad audience in part by using plain English in simple, reader-friendly, and understandable language. At the same time, while *American Law 101* provides some of the core principles underlying the American legal system in a straightforward way, its scope and mandate may not allow for each possible exception to be fully covered.

American Law 101's substance and style include the following:

- An easy-to-read and succinct primer on some of the core law concepts covered in many American law schools
- A comprehensive, quick, and easy-to-understand American law primer geared for a very broad audience—lawyers, non-lawyers, students, and administrators, domestically and internationally, in the legal profession and marketplace—as an introduction, summary, or review of important American law principles
- Concepts and terms explained simply using plain English with minimal use of jargon, legalese, American colloquialisms, cultural and sports references, slang, and other related references
- Short executive summary sections accompanying each chapter as useful wrap-ups
- Simple diagrams and explanations conveying concepts clearly and concisely

As with all written works, *American Law 101* has been helped by other publications related to and preceding it. *The Unofficial Guide to Legal Studies in the U.S. for Foreign Lawyers* (ABA 2012) is a very well-produced ABA publication focusing on the American law school experience, separate from covering core American law concepts.

Law 101: Everything You Need to Know About American Law (OUP 2010) is another useful book that covers American law concepts and topics at a minute, detailed, and technical level, which could be appropriate for a semester-long course. *American Law and Legal Systems* (Pearson 2011) is another full and formal academic text rather than a quick and easy primer on American law. In terms of writing like an American lawyer, *Plain English for Lawyers* (Carolina Academic Press 2005) is an excellent resource. Finally, *How Law Students Should Think* (Amazon Digital Services, Inc. 2011) is an insightful, complementary resource for those who want to understand how to succeed in the potentially competitive environment of some American law schools. Readers interested in learning more in depth and formally about American legal concepts, or the American law school experience, should certainly refer to some or all of the above publications, which are complementary but distinguishable from this book.

I am grateful for the opportunity afforded to me by the ABA to write *American Law 101*. Any one book attempting to encapsulate a field as intricate, influential, and dynamic as the American legal system has a daunting mandate. This book therefore should represent the beginning, not the end, of the reader's roadmap to American law.

Moreover, any mistakes in this book are my own.

As you read this book's pages, I hope that *American Law 101* sheds at least a small light on your road towards a better understanding of the American legal system—and the legal professionals working in it—domestically and internationally.

HOW TO THINK LIKE AN AMERICAN LAWYER

How do American (U.S.-licensed) lawyers think? What is the objective of American law schools? The two questions are interrelated. American law school education aspires to teach students how to think like a lawyer. For many students, this mandate is murky. Many of them arrive at law school with the assumption that the objective of a U.S. law school is to teach the law. But is it?

The short answer is yes and no. Yes, American law schools do teach the law, but the instruction of the law is often equally valued with how to use the law. To use the law, a future American lawyer must know not only what the law is, but also how to use and apply the law. Put simply, the difference is similar to the difference in understanding and memorizing the rules of a game versus knowing the process and strategy of how to play the game.

As a modern 21st century analogy of explaining the thinking process and how it relates to the American legal system, think of the American legal system—including the law itself within this legal system—as the system's hardware. The ability and skill set to process and effectively leverage this system in a value-added way is thinking like a lawyer, which represents the American lawyer's software.

So how do American lawyers think? American lawyers think through a structured analytical approach that allows them to filter vast types of relevant and irrelevant information and data to ultimately arrive at a recommended course of action vis-à-vis this structured analysis.

The IRAC approach reflects one, but not all, of the main ways that American lawyers think. The IRAC legal method is described as follows:

- **I**ssue: Legal question is presented.
- **R**ule (of law): Rule of law that applies to the Issue is determined.
- **A**pply: Rule (of law) is applied to the case's specific facts.
- **C**onclusion: A yes or no answer to the Issue is given.

Each of the IRAC components can generally be written in one sentence. The exception is for the Apply section, which can be anywhere from several sentences to several paragraphs.

The IRAC analytical framework can be and is used in different ways. It is generally used to synthesize and summarize a legal case in a clear, succinct, and efficient way. With IRAC, a legal case of either 10 or 10,000 words can generally be condensed to a simple page or two written in plain English (more on this topic later). This process helps because condensing the legal case requires prioritizing and editing case sections that are relatively less important (a form of proactive legal learning). This, in turn, requires that the reader must know the material, not just be able to read and understand the material (a form of passive legal learning). The IRAC process is also beneficial after the fact, because the IRAC version of the legal case only has the bare essentials of the case, which is a clear and concise reference point for law students and/or legal professionals.

Let's now look at each of the specific parts of the IRAC process.

Issue

The Issue is the legal question presented (and, as such, to be analyzed and answered). The Issue is essentially the leader of the IRAC team. This is because all of the other IRAC components (Rule, Apply, and Conclusion) directly relate to the Issue. So, if the Issue is correct, this increases the chances of the other sections also being correct. If the Issue is partially or completely incorrect, then the chances are relatively high that the IRAC in whole and in its component parts will also be partially or completely incorrect, which is not a good thing.

Because the Issue is the first IRAC component, the IRAC method is issue-driven. This is also in part why American law schools, lawyers, and other legal professionals are also issue-driven. It is thus critically important to focus on and find the correct Issue(s) in the American lawyer's legal analysis. This is a very important point, and it cannot be stressed enough.

With the IRAC method, one key takeaway is to place a great deal of focus on the Issue, generally and specifically, in terms of word choice. As lawyers who follow a logical scientific process, the importance of asking the right questions can often apply to American law, the legal method related to thinking about the law, and general lawyering.

In terms of textual writing and word choice for the Issue, generally the word "whether" should be the first or one of the first trigger words in the sentence. Specifically, the Issue can be written as either "The issue is whether . . ." or more directly "Whether . . ." Other words with similar meanings and functionality can also be used, but at least for the early stages of understanding the IRAC process and how American lawyers think, staying consistent and focused on the word "whether" will have more benefits than drawbacks.

In your early days of learning how to IRAC a law case, several issues may seem appropriate. As a general rule, which may have exceptions, the more specific the Issue is, the more likely it is to be exact. Think of hitting the right Issue like a game of archery. The archer's goal in the game is to maximize her point total, with more points earned by being closer to the exact center of the target. Maximizing points is most efficiently done by hitting a bull's-eye, because it gives the archer maximum points for the shot. In the same way, the goal for the IRAC method should be to hit an Issue that scores a bull's-eye—that is, an Issue that is finely targeted to hit the exact center of the target, not just shot anywhere broadly or approximately around it.

For example, which of the following issues would be better?

A: The issue is whether a contract existed between Mr. and Mrs. Smith.

B: The issue is whether Mrs. Smith accepted Mr. Smith's offer to sell Mr. Smith's car to Mrs. Smith for $20,000.

Both issues relate to contracts (discussed in Chapters 3 and 4). As a result, both issues are at least partially correct, but relatively speaking, Answer B is more exact than Answer A (assuming that the facts reflect the latter half of Answer B related to a contractual offer and acceptance of a car for a $20,000 sale and purchase price between Mr. and Mrs. Smith). Note also that the chosen Issue was written in one sentence.

Rule (of Law)

The Rule of law is the specific "black letter law" that directly and specifically applies to the Issue. The source of the Rule can be from various sources, ranging from court decisions to statutes. In terms of textual writing and word choice, the Rule should generally begin with the words, "The general rule is . . ." Much like the Issue, the Rule should ideally be written in one sentence. Also like the Issue, the Rule should be as exact and directly applicable to the Issue as possible.

Let's look at the previous example with Mr. and Mrs. Smith. Which of the following two Rules (of law) would be better?

A: The general rule is that a valid offer and acceptance are needed to reflect mutual assent within a contract.

B: The general rule is that a "meeting of the minds" must exist within a contract.

Much like with the previous choices related to choosing the best Issue, the two choices for choosing the best Rule both seem at least somewhat correct. The gap between the two answers here is small. Answer B relates to a famous contract law passage, "meeting of the minds," which is often seen as evidence of mutual assent (more on this in the book's Contracts chapters), but Answer A hits closer to the bull's-eye zone by incorporating offer and acceptance, which are predecessors to mutual assent (that is, offer and acceptance must first exist to subsequently have mutual assent). Assuming that offer and acceptance components existed in the case facts, Answer A would be more exact and directly related to the Issue. As a result, in this example, Answer A is the better Rule.

Apply

The Apply section synthesizes the Rule of law to the Issue and case facts. In other words, it applies the Rule, which is meant to be used in a variety of factual contexts, to the specific facts presented. This is done as part of the IRAC analytical framework to arrive at the Conclusion. Because the facts, Issue, and Rule are all synthesized and integrated in the Apply section, each of these components is often included in this section. This is also why the Apply section is typically not just one sentence, as is often the case with the Issue, Rule, and Conclusion.

In terms of textual writing and word choice, the first term that is generally used is either, "Here in this case . . ." or more directly, "Here . . .". This one word, much like with "whether" (Issue) and "general rule" (Rule), is an important, purposeful word choice that signals this section is definitively the Apply section of the IRAC analysis. Try also to use the word "because" as a clear signal to the reader that you are forming a direct link between two things, such as the facts and Rule. Such purposeful word choice, despite its brevity and succinctness, is what defines American lawyers (and, increasingly, non-American lawyers worldwide). Put simply, words matter, and words are key components of the lawyer's craft and profession.

Which of the two following answers would generally be considered better?

A: Here, Mr. and Mrs. Smith discussed buying property. Mr. Smith offered a price, although it was unclear whether Mrs. Smith agreed on the price.

B: Here, Mr. and Mrs. Smith discussed the possible sale and purchase of Mr. Smith's car. After some discussion, Mr. Smith offered to sell his car for $20,000. Mrs. Smith laughed when hearing this, and was silent thereafter. The general rule is that both a valid offer and acceptance are needed to form mutual assent in a contract. Neither laughter nor silence constitutes a valid acceptance. Therefore, neither valid acceptance nor mutual assent existed in this case because Mrs. Smith did not express a clear intent to accept Mr. Smith's $20,000 car sale.

Answer A is short but arguably not succinct because it lacks certain key details. For instance, the term "property" could instead have been more specifically written as "Mr. Smith's car" or simply as "car." The general term "price" could instead have been more specifically written as "$20,000," and Mrs. Smith's reaction to Mr. Smith's offer by laughing and then staying silent could also have been used. All such textual changes could have been done without adding much if any unneeded wording. Answer B is lengthier but arguably better because it effectively incorporates key facts, such as the $20,000 offered car sale price as well as Mrs. Smith's action and inaction of laughter and silence, respectively, after hearing Mr. Smith's suggested car sale price. As a result, relatively speaking, Answer B is the better answer.

Conclusion

The Conclusion section succinctly answers the Issue (legal question raised). It represents the final outcome based on the IRAC's analytical framework. In terms of textual writing and word choice, the Conclusion should generally begin with a "Yes" or "No" directly followed by the Issue (written in a statement rather than question form). Put simply, the conclusion's written structure would be: "[YES]/[NO], [ISSUE]."

As a final example related to IRAC, which of the following two answers would be better?

A: No, mutual assent did not exist between Mr. and Mrs. Smith related to Mr. Smith's car.

B: The conclusion for this case depends on several criteria, which this court has fully considered, as would be the case in a contractual dispute of this nature, as seen in this particular considered case. As such, and given the facts in this case, and considering the totality of the circumstances, including Mr. and Mrs. Smith's intent and actions related to the said property, it can be said that, for legal purposes under the purview of this court, and the powers vested in it, that mutual assent did not exist due to most notably Mrs. Smith's action and inaction in reaction to Mr. Smith's action.

Unlike the previous example, the gap between Answers A and B is wider. For the layperson (nonlegal expert or nonlawyer), Answer B may have the look and feel of seeming more legal. After all, it has long sentences with obtuse wording that seems a bit indecipherable, but does legalese always equate to legal sense? No, not always.

For the answer choices, Answer B's style and substance begins to resemble more of the beginning of a legal treatise than a simple Conclusion section, whereas Answer A accomplishes in one sentence what Answer B barely accomplishes or does not accomplish in several lengthy sentences. So Answer A is better in terms of grammatical style. In terms of legal substance, Answer A also accomplishes in one sentence what Answer B took several sentences to declare in terms of zooming in on the key terminology of offer, acceptance, and mutual acceptance. As a result, Answer A is generally considered the better answer.

This section discussed the IRAC analytical framework to provide not only an effective means to synthesize cases but also a sense of how American lawyers think. While textual wording and word choice writing frameworks were provided specific to the IRAC analytical framework, the next section discusses in more detail how American lawyers write.

Contrary to what many people may think, the modern trend in American law schools and the legal profession is toward writing in plain English. The next section discusses plain English and provides basic strategies combined with examples.

Plain English

How do American lawyers write? This question also links to how American lawyers think. The modern trend is for lawyers, and thus law students, to write in plain English and to not use writing that incorporates a lot of legal jargon.

The rationale for this approach is that writing in plain English is a sign of effective legal writing. Plain English is clear and concise language without the use of unnecessary legal jargon. Plain English is more appealing to a wider audience, because it uses everyday terms to the greatest extent possible rather than relying on technical terminology. Put another way, plain English is more reader friendly. Being more reader friendly is important, because legal opinions should ideally be accessible for the general public—including the layperson—as well as legal professionals.

Directly reflecting this principle, some U.S. states now require that certain contracts be written in plain English, which could include rental agreements between landlords and tenants. Because many actual and potential tenants who sign such agreements are presumed to be nonlegal experts, writing agreements in plain English helps to make them more understandable and lower the chances of one side taking advantage of another side.

Entire books have been written on how to write in plain English. One such book is Richard Wydick's *Plain English for Lawyers* (Carolina Academic Press, 1998). Rather than trying to duplicate this and other related works, following are some plain English rules and examples from Wydick's *Plain English for Lawyers* that may be useful in your legal writing while studying or practicing American law. Readers who are interested in improving their legal writing skills should certainly read Wydick's entire book, which has many more rules and examples. The following are the top 10 rules for writing in plain English:

1. Delete surplus words
2. Use a Subject-Verb-Object sentence structure
3. Use base verbs (not nominalizations)
4. Use the active voice
5. Keep sentences short
6. Use bullet points and tabs (when conveying mass information)
7. Put modifying words next to the words being modified

8. Prefer the singular number and the present tense
9. Use familiar and succinct words (avoiding lawyerisms)
10. Avoid sexist language

Plain English Rule 1: Delete Surplus Words

Example (without plain English): In many instances, insofar as the jurors are concerned, the jury instructions are not understandable because they are too poorly written.

Example (with plain English): Often jury instructions are too poorly written for the jurors to understand.

Plain English Rule 2: Use a Subject-Verb-Object sentence structure

Example (without plain English): There were no reasons offered by the court for denying punitive damages.

Example (with plain English): The court offered no reasons for denying punitive damages.

Plain English Rule 3: Use base verbs (not nominalizations)

Example (without plain English): We are in agreement with your position, but if it is your intention to cause delay, we will stand in opposition to you.

Example (with plain English): We agree with your position, but if you intend to cause delay, we will oppose you.

Plain English Rule 4: Use the active voice

Example (without plain English): This agreement may be terminated by either party by defendant manufacturers, and it was agreed that all sales would be made at list prices or above.

Example (with plain English): Either party may terminate this agreement by giving 30 days' notice to the other party.

Plain English Rule 5: Keep sentences short

Example (without plain English): While there are instances in which consumer abuse and exploitation result from advertising that is false, misleading, or irrelevant, it does not necessarily follow that these cases need to be remedied by governmental intervention in the marketplace, because it is possible for consumers' interests to be protected through resort to the courts, either by consumers themselves or by those competing sellers who see their market shares decline in the face of inroads based on such advertising.

Example (with plain English): Consumers are sometimes abused and exploited by false, misleading, or irrelevant advertising, but that does not necessarily require the government to intrude into the marketplace. Consumers themselves can go to court, as can competing sellers who lose business because of such advertising.

Plain English Rule 6: Use bullet points and tabs (when conveying mass information)

Example (without plain English): Venue would be proper, unless the claim is framed as a federal question, in the Southern District of New York, if that is where the plaintiff resides, or in the Eastern District of California, assuming that the defendant does business in that judicial district, or in the Northern District of Illinois, if that turns out to be the place where the events in question happened.

Example (with plain English): Unless the claim is framed as a federal question, venue would be proper in any of these judicial districts:

- The Southern District of New York, if the plaintiff resides there; or
- The Eastern District of California, if the defendant does business there; or
- The Northern District of Illinois, if the events in question took place there.

Plain English Rule 7: Put modifying words next to the words being modified

Example (without plain English): The plaintiff's pain can be alleviated only by expensive therapy.

Example (with plain English): Only expensive therapy can alleviate the plaintiff's pain.

Plain English Rule 8: Prefer the singular number and the present tense

Example (without plain English): Persons must not discharge firearms inside city limits.

Example (with plain English): A person must not discharge a firearm inside city limits.

Plain English Rule 9: Use familiar and succinct words (avoiding lawyerisms)

Example (without plain English): This agreement, unless revocation has occurred at an earlier date, shall expire on November 11, 2016.

Example (with plain English): Unless sooner revoked, this agreement expires on November 11, 2016.

Plain English Rule 10: Avoid sexist language

Example (without plain English): Blue-collar work involving heavy lifting and construction requires a manly effort, whereby a judge will surely apply a reasonable man's legal standard to the case.

Example (with plain English): Blue-collar work involving heavy lifting and construction requires physically strenuous effort, whereby a judge will surely apply a reasonable person's legal standard to the case.

Summary

To understand the hardware of the American legal system, the software of the American legal system and its legal professionals must first be examined in terms of the thinking process underlying it. So how does an American lawyer think? Although many factors exist, American lawyers are generally driven by issues (legal questions) in a particular case or lawsuit.

The IRAC—Issue, Rule (of law), Apply, and Conclusion—legal method used by many law students and legal professionals incorporates the Issue component as the lead component. The Rule (of law) in the IRAC system requires the writer—whether a law student or legal professional—to know and write the general rule of law specifically related to the issue. The Apply section synthesizes and incorporates the general rule with the facts in the case, and the Conclusion section provides a clear yes or no answer to the issue presented.

How American lawyers write is a direct reflection of how American lawyers think. The modern trend in American law is to write in plain English. Several rules are provided in this chapter as a general framework on how American lawyers and other legal professionals write for their domestic and increasingly global audience.

THE AMERICAN LEGAL SYSTEM MADE EASY

Chapter 1 discussed the software of the American lawyer (i.e., in terms of the thinking process operating within the minds of U.S.-licensed legal professionals). This chapter, in contrast, examines the hardware in terms of the conceptual component parts within the software of the American lawyer and legal system. Specifically, the hardware is based in part on the black letter law embedded within the American legal infrastructure, which this chapter will now briefly overview.

Common Law Versus Other Domestic Laws

American law is based on common law from the United Kingdom as one of its core legal pillars (which is then buttressed by, among other sources, the U.S. Constitution, court cases, statutes, restatements, decrees, treatises, and various other rules and regulations).

Common law follows the principle of stare decisis (Latin, meaning "stand by your decision"). Stare decisis is a legal principle stating that prior court decisions (e.g., holdings, conclusions, rulings) must be recognized as precedent case law. If a case is deemed a precedent case, then lower courts are compelled to rule in the same way as the precedent case. This applies only if the precedent case is binding or mandatory. The rationale for stare decisis and precedent cases is judicial efficiency, fairness to the parties, predictability, and a check and balance on arbitrary behavior.

In common law countries, juries and oral arguments by lawyers often can take a greater or more visible role compared to in civil law countries (which may not have jury trials), in which the judge can play a more central and prominent role (of course, exceptions can exist).

Examples of jurisdictions that use the common law system include the following:

- United Kingdom except Scotland
- United States except Louisiana
- Ireland
- Former British colony and/or Commonwealth territories/countries, including India except Goa, Australia, New Zealand, Singapore, and Canada except Quebec
- Pakistan
- Bangladesh

In contrast, generally under civil law (derived from the French-German legal tradition), statutes and other similar legal sources represent relatively greater legal authority than does case law. Under civil law, neither precedent cases nor stare decisis exist. The rationale for this is greater judicial freedom to decide cases on a case-by-case basis. Some people argue, however, that this system may come at the cost of less predictability and consistency regarding case law conclusions (with similar legal issues and/or facts).

Examples of jurisdictions that use the civil law system include the following:

- Most European Union (EU) nations, including Germany and France where civil law was derived, but not the United Kingdom, Ireland, or Cyprus
- Most of continental Latin America except Guyana and Belize
- Congo
- Azerbaijan
- Iraq
- Russia
- Turkey
- Egypt
- Madagascar
- Lebanon
- Switzerland
- Indonesia
- Vietnam
- Thailand

The factors used in determining whether to apply stare decisis include the following:

- Similarity of legal issue(s)/legal principle(s)
- Whether the precedent case was ruled on by a court recognized as a leading one in the relevant subject area

- Whether the precedent case was well-reasoned and articulated (in the court's legal opinion)
- Whether the precedent case was issued from a court in the same jurisdiction
- Whether the precedent case was issued from a higher-level court

Although these factors are often considered to determine whether a case is a precedent case, thus representing a binding and mandatory legal source, a court may not be required to follow:

- Secondary legal sources (i.e., nonprecedent cases, not related to the U.S. Constitution, and the like; see the following paragraph for further specifics)
- Cases that do not align with these factors to determine the precedential value of a case

Two main types of legal sources exist in American law: primary and secondary.

1. Primary legal sources include the following:
   - U.S. Constitution
   - Statutes
   - Rules, regulations, and orders
   - Executive orders and proclamations
   - Case law
2. Secondary legal sources include the following:
   - Treatises
   - Restatements
   - Law review journals
   - *American Law Reports*
   - Hornbooks
   - Legal encyclopedias

A general hierarchy also exists in which federal legal sources are weighed more heavily than state legal sources:

A. Federal Legal Sources
   - U.S. Constitution
   - Federal statutes and treaties
   - Federal rules and regulations
   - Federal cases

B. State Legal Sources
   - State constitutions
   - State statutes

- State rules and regulations
- State law cases

From this list, two interesting points arise: (1) the U.S. Constitution represents the supreme law of the land, and (2) a federal supremacy rule applies. This means that federal sources are generally higher than state sources in the legal source hierarchy. This is important to know for both academics and practitioners to determine what legal source should be given greater weight relative to others, which can help in the legal strategy process.

State Law

Although the United States is one country, from a legal perspective, each individual state within it has a certain level of discretion to determine what types of laws best fit that particular state's set of circumstances. The concept of dualism, in which sources of law exist dually at both the federal and state level, is based in part on the view that decentralization of power is needed. The intent of dualism was to provide greater security that one central source of authority would not become overly powerful—as was the case with England at the time of the founding of the United States.

Furthermore, as Chapter 6 discusses in greater detail regarding Constitutional Law, the U.S. Constitution (the nation's highest legal authority) has embedded in it a concept known as the enumerated powers doctrine. In the enumerated powers doctrine, the federal government has only those powers expressly conveyed to it under the Constitution (under Article I, Section 8), with all other remaining powers generally belonging to the states.

Thus, state laws are actually much more widely encompassing than many people from non–common law countries would expect. With this in mind, each specific state's law can vary and be different from other state laws. Although diversity exists, many state laws are based on certain standardized laws.

Examples of standardized laws that state law can be based on include the following:

- Restatements of law, which are used to provide clarity on certain law matters
  - Prepared by the American Law Institute (ALI)
  - Represents secondary (nonprimary) legal source/authority
- Uniform acts/Uniform codes, such as the Uniform Commercial Code, or UCC, relating to contract law
  - Drafted by the Uniform Law Commissioners
  - Body of lawyers and other legal professionals whose objective is to standardize laws across the various U.S. states
  - Offered as legal models, which each state can ratify in whole or in part

- Model penal code (MPC), relating to criminal law matters
  - Prepared by the ALI, much like restatements
  - Objective of updating and standardizing penal law across the various U.S. states
  - MPC represents what the ALI deems as the best rules for the U.S. penal system

Much like the dual federal-state level of legal sources, a similar dual system of federal-state court systems exists. Consistent with the principle of federalism, federal courts rank higher in the judicial court hierarchy relative to state courts.

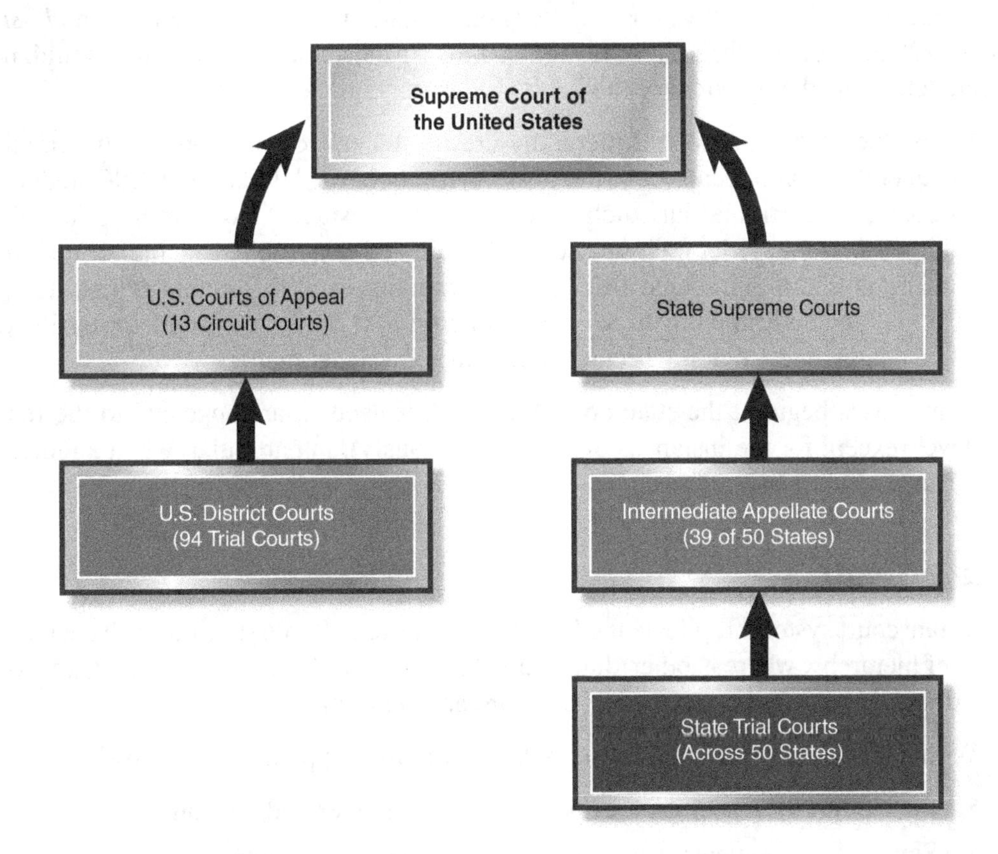

The Federal Court hierarchy (from highest to lowest) is as follows:

- U.S. Supreme Court
- Circuit courts
- District courts

Federal courts consider the following legal sources:

- Federal (nonstate) statutory issues

- Diversity cases, such as cases involving parties from two different states
- Cases in which the United States is a party as plaintiff or defendant
- Other cases as specified by law (e.g., admiralty, antitrust, maritime)
- Removal jurisdiction cases, in which the defendant requests the case to be heard by a federal, rather than a state, court in the same district

The U.S. Supreme Court (USSC) is the highest court in the United States. The U.S. Supreme Court generally hears cases based on appeal (when certiorari—or in plain English, review—is granted to review the case). In other words, the USSC is only in rare circumstances the court of first instance having original jurisdiction over a case. Of course, exceptions exist when an issue is particularly urgent. For instance, the *Bush v. Gore* (2000) case was heard by the USSC at first instance because its ruling could, in effect, determine the outcome of the 2000 U.S. presidential election.

Below the USSC in judicial hierarchy are the federal circuit courts. The circuit courts generally hear appeals from the lower district courts. Unlike the USSC, federal circuit courts have original jurisdiction (court of first instance) over orders of certain federal agencies. The federal circuit courts are divided geographically into 13 circuit courts. Circuit courts numbered from 1 to 13 encompass all of the states (including Hawaii), with an additional district for Washington D.C. (which is a federal territory, not a U.S. state), and a federal circuit for certain specialized matters.

Many cases begin at the state court level and, if needed, are appealed to the federal level (except for the instances discussed previously), in particular, when a federal (rather than a state) issue arises.

State Courts

Most state court systems replicate the federal court system. Some state courts have three levels of hierarchy, whereas other state courts have two levels of hierarchy. Regardless, each state court has its own rules of procedure and set of practices.

With a three-level state court system, the hierarchy is typically the following:

- State Supreme Court: Hears appeals from state intermediate court
- State court of appeals: Hears appeals from lower trial court
- State trial court: Conducts fact-finding as well as ruling on the legal issue(s) presented

State courts usually can review almost any case, but exceptions exist, such as where jurisdiction is precluded by (1) federal statute; (2) the U.S. Constitution; or (3) other legal source, expressly (e.g., admiralty, patent, copyright) or implicitly (e.g., antitrust damages and injunction).

American Judicial System

The United States has three branches of government: (1) the legislative branch (the Congress, which is composed of the Senate and House of Representatives); (2) the executive branch (including the U.S. President), and (3) the judicial branch (including the USSC and other courts). The three branches of government are based on the concept of checks and balances, so that each branch of government does not become too powerful relative to the other two branches.

Related terms are defined as follows:

- Congress: Bicameral institution that refers to the Senate and the House of Representatives
- House of Representatives:
    - Referred to as the lower house (because the legislative process typically begins here and then proceeds to the Senate).
    - The number of Representatives is based on the population of each state (thus, the larger and more populated states—such as California, Texas, and New York—generally have more Representatives).
    - House representatives are elected to two-year terms and can be reelected continuously.
- Senate:
    - Referred to as the higher chamber (because the Senate is the second chamber in the legislative process).
    - Two senators are elected from each of the 50 states (regardless of a state's population).
    - Senators are elected to six-year terms with the possibility of reelections.
- Government lawyers:
    - Prosecutor: A government attorney who prepares and conducts the prosecution of the accused party
    - District Attorney (DA) (or county prosecutor): A government prosecutor representing a particular state
    - United States (U.S.) Attorney: A federal prosecutor representing the United States for certain federal districts

An example of checks and balances in practice could involve an impeachment proceeding against the executive branch. An attempt to impeach the U.S. President (executive branch), for instance, would involve the legislative branch placing a check and balance on the executive branch by arguing, among other things, that certain actions of the presidency allegedly violated the U.S. Constitution. The judicial branch (federal courts) can serve as a check and balance if it decides to review the acts of the legislative branch in terms of constitutionality (i.e., to determine whether an act by the legislative branch allegedly violated the U.S. Constitution, which all three branches must abide by). The federal courts can also review the actions of federal administrative agencies. At the same time, the legislative branch (Congress) can review and overrule court precedent under its designated Congressional authority.

The American legal system can appear diverse and complex. With the overview provided in this chapter, it is hoped that readers have a better understanding and greater clarity regarding the hardware of American law. This understanding of the American legal infrastructure will help, as the next chapters will fill in the landscape—section by section—that will culminate into a panoramic primer of American law.

The reading and understanding of cases is important in most, if not all, jurisdictions in the world. The U.S. legal system, which is based on the common law system of England, treats case law (law based on the interpretation of cases by the judiciary) as especially important. This is based on the previously mentioned concept of stare decisis. Under stare decisis, lower courts often must (as opposed to can) rule and conclude the case in a manner consistent with higher courts in the same jurisdiction regarding previous cases with similar facts and issues (which links back to the IRAC legal thinking process covered earlier in Chapter 1).

The American legal system's main rationale for stare decisis is consistency and greater foreseeability of how similar cases may be concluded by the courts. However, with benefits come drawbacks. With stare decisis, the drawback is less judicial discretion afforded to the courts and judges in an effort to treat each dispute on a case-by-case basis. What is considered as the drawback of the common law system under stare decisis is often viewed as the benefit of the civil law system, in which stare decisis does not apply. This thus gives greater judicial discretion to the courts, at the potential cost of inconsistent judicial conclusions even within the same jurisdiction.

So which domestic legal system among the two is better: common law or civil law? When students and even practitioners pose this question, a common first answer is that each system has both benefits and costs (as analyzed here), and it is incumbent upon each jurisdiction to determine which system makes the most sense, all things considered. The other answer is that an increasing convergent trend is now occurring, whereby legal practitioners from both common and civil legal traditions often tend to think more similarly now than in the past, particularly in commercial transactions and dealings. This convergence may be in part a result of globalization, technological advancements, and students studying internationally—creating a greater exposure and knowledge base of the common law tradition (as well as civil law and other domestic legal traditions, such as Islamic law). (See the Appendices for further specifics on the American court system.)

To understand the American legal system, legal cases reflecting case law must be understood in great detail. This is especially critical given the importance of stare decisis and precedent cases in American law, as discussed earlier. Because of the importance of case law and understanding cases, the next section provides a more detailed glimpse into the main elements of a case within the American judicial system, including a method of how to read and brief a case—a vital skill set for both the study and practice of American law.

How to Read and Brief a Case

With the high level of importance given to stare decisis and precedent cases underlying American law, a fundamental knowledge of how to understand and brief a U.S. case is critically important. This is true as a law student as well as a law practitioner who aspires to gain a greater understanding of American law.

To begin, most court decisions are published, both at the federal and state level. The court issuing the opinion often has the discretion in deciding whether to publish an opinion it has rendered.

Specific case elements exist in a typical case brief, which include the following:

- Case Name and its citation to find and/or reference the case
- Author of the Opinion (the Opinion is the court's ruling/decision): Generally, the person who authors a legal opinion is a judge or arbitrator (the concept and role of arbitrators is discussed in greater detail in Chapter 10).
- Opinion, which generally includes:
  - Case Facts and relevant procedural history of the case, such as past appeals and rulings
  - Court Conclusion, also referred to as the case's holding
  - Reasoning: Detailing the rationale, arguments, and other factors considered by the court
  - Disposition: Court action based on the court's ruling/conclusion (e.g., reversed, affirmed, remanded.)

The case caption can be thought of as a title for a case. Example: *Brown v. Board of Education*, 347 U.S. 483 (1954). The case caption includes the parties, case citation (court name, law book where the opinion is published), and year of the court's conclusion. In terms of formality of writing for a case caption, the party names to the dispute are italicized and/or underlined (the example has the party names italicized). The remaining case caption (e.g., citation/reporter details, year that the decision was rendered, and other related details) generally is not italicized or underlined.

Reporters

Cases that are published are included in publications called reporters. Each reporter has a volume number and page numbers. Some reporters are published by the state, while some are published by commercial institutions. For the case citation/reporter relating to the previous example, the case would be found in volume 347 of the *United States Reports* on page 483.

Judicial Titles

The author of the court opinion, as mentioned, is typically a judge. In this case, the judge, in his or her capacity as legal opinion author (for the majority or minority opinion), is written at the top of the legal opinion, as follows:

Example: "Hand, J." refers to Judge Hand.

Example: "Holmes J." is Justice Holmes.

Some jurisdictions use terms other than "judge," albeit referring to the same judicial decision-rendering role:

Example: "Jackson, C." refers to Chancellor Jackson.

Example: "Jackson, V.C." refers to Vice-Chancellor Jackson.

Example: "Jackson, C.J." refers to Chief Judge Jackson.

Party Names

In a civil (noncriminal) case, the party initiating the lawsuit is the plaintiff, and the party defending against the plaintiff's lawsuit is the defendant (not coincidentally, the term "defendant" has the term "defend" embedded in it). In criminal (noncivil) cases, the party initiating the lawsuit is referred to as the state (or similar terminology), because the interests of the state (or other relevantly named party initiating the lawsuit) are presumed greater than one individual (such as by a plaintiff in a civil law case).

The plaintiffs (or state) are usually the first party listed in the caption. For the previous caption example, Brown is the plaintiff at the initial stage (prior to an appeal, if an appeal is rendered). If a case is heard on appeal (in which a case is heard for the second time or more), then the party initiating the appeal is called the appellant. The party defending against the appellant's lawsuit on appeal is called the appellee. Thus, as an example, if the Board of Education in the previous example appealed, then the Board of Education would be the first named party in the caption of the appealed case (rather than second, as was the case in the original lawsuit example).

The court's conclusion or ruling is the court's legal opinion and the rationale given for reaching a particular judgment, finding, or conclusion. Underneath the broad term of legal opinion, several specific subsets of opinions exist. A concurring opinion is an opinion rendered by a judge who would have reached the same conclusion as the majority opinion, but for a different reason (i.e., same destination, but would have chosen a different route to get to the destination). A plurality opinion is an opinion agreed on by less than the majority of the judges (assuming a panel of judges), but the opinion agrees with the majority opinion's conclusion. A dissenting opinion is an opinion by one or more judges who disagree with the majority opinion's conclusion.

The parties to a lawsuit (at the initial trial court level) include the following:

- Plaintiff: Party initiating the lawsuit
- Defendant: Party defending against the lawsuit (legal action by plaintiff)
- Counterclaimant: Defendant's counterclaim against the plaintiff
- Cross-claimant: Defendant bringing a lawsuit against a third party, typically with a view that the introduced third party was at least partially responsible/liable for owed damages to plaintiff
- Third-party defendant: Party defending against a cross-claim for alleged damages owed to plaintiff
- Intervenor: Interested party participating in litigation with the court's permission

The parties to a lawsuit (at the noninitial appellate court level) include the following:

- Appellant: Party appealing a lower court's ruling (usually the unsuccessful party in the previous lawsuit)
- Appellee: Party defending against the appellant's actions
- Petitioner: Party challenging action, usually in an agency context
- Respondent: Party defending against petitioner's actions, usually in an agency context
- Intervenor: Same as intervenor at the trial court level
- Amicus curiae ("friend of the court"): Party given court permission to participate in the case
- U.S. Solicitor: Government attorney representing the United States

The parties to a lawsuit (at the highest U.S. Supreme Court level) include the following:

- Petitioner: Party seeking the Supreme Court's review, arguing for the rejection of the lower court's decision
- Respondent: Party opposing the Supreme Court's review, arguing that the lower court's decision does not warrant review, because the lower court's conclusion and rationale are legally valid
- Intervenor: Same as intervenor at the trial/appellate court level
- Amicus curiae: Same as at the appeals court level
- U.S. Solicitor: Government attorney representing the United States

Court Dispositions—General

- Order: Court resolution of a motion (filed by one of the parties)
- Affirmation: Court's decision to uphold the lower court's ruling
- Reversal: Court's rejection of the lower court's ruling
- Remand: Court order to return the case to the lower court (or agency) for further factual findings, or for other resolution in conformity with the appellate court's decision
- Vacate: Court rejection of the lower court's ruling, with an order to set aside and render the lower court's ruling as null and void
- Modification: Court's affirmation of part of the lower court's decision, with an ordered modification to the opinion

Court Dispositions—Appellate Courts

- En Banc Opinion:
  - Represents an opinion by all members of the court, not just a certain number (panel) of sitting judges, to hear a particular case
  - Generally represents a rare exception rather than the norm
  - Usually seen in issues of extreme importance

Court Disposition—Supreme Court

- Plurality Opinion:
  - An opinion that more judges sign than any concurring opinion
  - Does not constitute a majority opinion
  - Does not have the force of precedent, because it is not a result of a majority opinion
- Certiorari Granted:
  - Grant of discretionary review by the U.S. Supreme Court (often considered the exception rather than the norm because the Supreme Court is unable to grant certiorari to most cases given its limited time and resources)
  - Does not reverse or directly affect lower court rulings
- Certiorari Denied:
  - U.S. Supreme Court's decision to reject discretionary review of a particular lower court ruling
  - Does not generally have precedential effect

In most legal opinions, part of the court's decision may include analysis and language that may not directly be necessary to reach the court's resolution of the legal issue. This part of the case is referred to as dictum. Dictum is not the court's holding.

In other words, dictum is related, but separate from, the court's holding. Given that dictum is not part of a court's holding, stare decisis does not apply. It may be difficult to distinguish a court's dictum from its holding. Still, dictum may be useful for future cases, because it is, at times, a signal or hint of how the court (or at least a judge in the court) may view a case in light of different legal issues or facts.

Summary

The American judicial system is based on British common law, which is then buttressed by, among other sources, the U.S. Constitution, court cases, statutes, restatements, decrees, treatises, and various other rules and regulations. The American legal system is composed of the U.S. Supreme Court, federal courts, and state courts. Within both federal and state courts, primary and secondary legal sources are considered. The U.S. Supreme Court is the highest land of the law. It can grant certiorari to select cases for various reasons, including whether the issue presented is urgent or of vital national interest. Generally, however, a lawsuit begins in state courts and then, as needed, is heard on appeal by federal (appellate-level) or state courts. Knowledge of the structure of the American judicial system is then furthered by understanding how to write and brief a law case, which is a vital skill set for law students and practitioners.

CONTRACTS I
(Offer and Acceptance)

Contracts are one of the core foundation courses for American law schools and legal professionals, for a variety of reasons. Perhaps one main reason is the seeming omnipresence of contracts beyond the classroom in practical settings—both in written and unwritten form—that are negotiated, entered into, and at times, terminated (or attempted to be terminated) within and outside of the United States. For instance, the non-U.S. lawyer may face American contract issues in his or her home jurisdiction as well as in the United States, ranging from entertainment law to construction contracts. Therefore, contracts are the first core hardware topic covered in *American Law 101*.

So what exactly is a contract? The definition of a contract is a promise or set of promises for the breach of which the law gives a remedy, or the performance of which the law in some way recognizes as a duty (definition from the Restatement (Second) of Contracts, American Law Institute (ALI), Article 1. Contracts can also be thought of as "an agreement between two or more people that creates an obligation to do or not to do a particular thing." The end result of a contract is the creation of a legal relationship involving rights and duties of legal persons, which can include individuals as well as corporate entities.

Several sources of law govern American law contracts, including the following:

- Common law (taken from English common law)
- Uniform Commercial Code (UCC)

    - UCC applies only to "sales of goods."
    - UCC was enacted in all 50 U.S. states and Washington, D.C.
- State of Louisiana (governed by civil, not common law) has enacted many UCC provisions, except for UCC, Article 2.
- Restatement of contracts (applies only if adopted by a specific state)

The jurisdiction (legal authority to hear a dispute) of many contracts is governed by state law and heard by state courts. Cases that may be heard by federal courts include, for instance, those contracts involving parties from different states or a citizen of a foreign nation.

To create a legally binding contract under American law, the following elements are necessary:

- Mutual Assent (the relevant parties "agree" and thus have an intent to enter into a contract), which is then subdivided into:
    - Offer
    - Acceptance
- Consideration (a "bargained-for exchange")
- Legality (that the agreement does not violate public policy)
- Capacity (that the party has contractual capacity to enter into the agreement)

An agreement generally only becomes a contract, rather than a mere agreement, if all of the required contract elements are met (the so-called birth of a contract). If any of the four elements are not met, then the agreement is generally not a contract, although exceptions can arise. This means that the parties will have a mere agreement, rather than a validly binding, and thus legally enforceable, contract.

As a result, if one of the parties violates one of the agreed-upon terms, a legal claim generally cannot be brought against the alleged breaching party with a mere agreement. However, with a contract that satisfies all of the required elements (after contract formation), the party that breached the contract may be liable for damages in a court of law. A contract breach occurs when one or more parties to a contract fails to perform some agreed-upon act and/or fails to comply with a duty imposed by law.

The next section focuses on the first contract element of mutual assent, specifically regarding offer and acceptance.

Offer and Acceptance

The next step is understanding what constitutes an offer under American law. A valid offer is the manifestation of willingness of a party to enter into a bargain. The party proposing the offer is the offeror. Under American law, a principle exists, which states that the "offeror is the master of his offer." Translated into plain English, this means that the offeror can create nearly any terms and conditions the offeror desires, assuming they do not violate other elements of the contract or other relevant laws in the jurisdiction.

A valid acceptance of the offer by the offeror is indicated by agreement to the offer terms. More formally, an acceptance under contract law is a manifestation of assent to the terms in a manner invited or required by the offer, remembering the notion that the offeror is the master of his offer.

How can offers be accepted? There are generally two ways an offer can be accepted: (1) through performance of a certain act, or (2) by a promise to perform in the future. Acceptance by performance requires that at least part of what the offer requests be performed. With the second acceptance method, by promise, the offeree must complete every act essential to the making of the promise.

What if the offer and/or acceptance is unclear? Does a contract exist? The short answer is generally no. In litigation (through a lawsuit), the court decides whether an offer and/or acceptance existed from a legal purview. When the courts make an analysis, they generally use the objective theory of contracts, which binds parties on what a "reasonable person" would understand of an explicit manifestation of the offer and/or acceptance at issue. As a result, implicit manifestations are generally not taken into account by the courts in determining whether an offer and/or acceptance existed. Thus, it is to the parties' benefit to make all understandings, terms, and conditions of the agreement as explicit as possible. If not, they will likely not be considered, and deemed as irrelevant, by the courts in determining whether or not a contract existed between the relevant parties. Put simply, to maximize the chance of an agreement being deemed as a validly binding contract, it is best to communicate offers and acceptances clearly and unequivocally.

Must all contracts be in writing and signed under American law? The short answer is no, unless the agreement stipulates otherwise. Generally, contracts can be in written or unwritten form, but if a dispute arises, the courts will stress test whether the contract truly reflects the intent of the parties, among other things. At the same time, one notable exception to this general rule is that certain agreements must be written under a concept known as the Statute of Frauds.

Although varying from state to state, the following contract types are normally required to be in writing (if not listed, then the possibility exists that the contract may not be required to be in writing):

- A contract to pay another's debt
- A contract in consideration of marriage
- A contract for the sale of a land interest
- A contract that is not to be performed within one year of the time it is made
- A contract for the sale of goods for $500 or more

The term "reasonable" is used often in American law. So what does "reasonable" mean exactly? Under American law, the term "reasonable" and the phrase "reasonable person" are works of legal art. In plain English, a "reasonable person" is what the fact finder (the judge or jury) would deem as reasonable. To add more clarity, think of the reasonable person as someone who is above the average person but not quite at the level of the perfect person, shown in the following graphic:

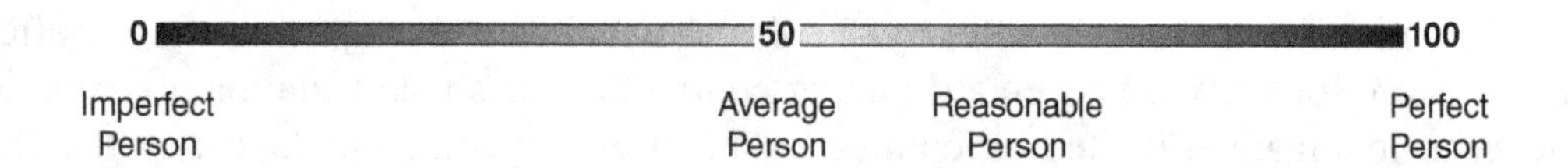

Here is an example of the reasonable person standard:

- **Case**: *Leonard v. PepsiCo, Inc.*, 88 F. Supp. 2d 116 (S.D.N.Y. 1999)
- **Facts**: Plaintiff John Leonard sued PepsiCo, Inc. alleging that the company had made an offer through a TV commercial it aired nationwide in the United States. PepsiCo.'s TV commercial featured a military fighter jet appearing as a young child won a redeemable product. The plaintiff alleged that the visual of the military fighter jet as a prize constituted a contractual offer, with an acceptance occurring when the relevant product was redeemed.
- **Issue**: Whether PepsiCo.'s TV commercial featuring a military fighter jet constituted an offer (applying a reasonable person's perspective)?
- **Conclusion**: No, PepsiCo.'s TV advertisement featuring a military fighter jet did not constitute an offer (applying a reasonable person's perspective).

One question related to this case is whether advertisements are offers. The general rule is that advertisements are usually not considered offers. What are advertisements then? From a legal purview, an advertisement is considered an "invitation to an offer" (one step before a valid offer). This is because an advertisement, generally speaking, is indefinite and incomplete. As a result, the act of a customer paying the price of a product is usually the offer. The store's acceptance occurs by accepting the money and handing the goods to the customer.

The exception to the general rule that advertisements are not offers can occur, creating a binding obligation if the advertisements made are clear, definite, and explicit offers, which leave nothing open for negotiation.

Here is an example of an invitation to offer case:

- **Case**: *Lefkowitz v. Great Minneapolis Surplus Store*, 251 Minn. 188, 86 N.W.2d 689 (1957)
- **Facts**: A store placed an advertisement in the newspaper on April 6, 1956, which had the following wording:
  - Saturday 9AM sharp
  - 3 brand new fur coats worth to $100
  - First come first served
  - $1 each

A male customer was the first person to arrive on that day. That customer requested the fur coat for $1. The store refused to sell the coat to the male customer, because the house rule was that the fur coats were for female customers only.

- **Facts (additional)**: The same store placed another advertisement in the newspaper on April 13, 1956, which had the following wording:
  - Saturday 9AM
  - 2 brand new pastel mink scarves
  - Selling for $89.50
  - $1 each
  - First come first served

The same male customer was again the first customer to arrive. The store again refused to sell him the advertised goods because he was a man. The male customer sued the store for refusing to accept his offer to buy the goods. The store argued that (1) the newspaper advertisement was only an "invitation to an offer" and not an offer in itself; and (2) the male customer offered to buy the goods, but the store simply rejected his offer to buy the goods.

- **Issue**: Whether the store's two advertisements constituted valid offers.
- **Conclusion**: Yes, the store's two advertisements did constitute a valid offer, rather than being deemed as an "invitation of an offer."
- **Rule (of law)**: An advertisement can constitute an offer, rather than a mere invitation to an offer, only if it is "a clear, definite, and explicit offer that leaves nothing open for negotiation."
- **Application (of rule to the facts)**: The store's advertisement was clear, definite, and explicit, and did not leave room for negotiation because (1) the exact day and time of the offer was given; (2) the exact location was given; (3) the exact price was given; and (4) the event was on a first-come, first-served basis.

Another aspect of American law contracts under common law is the mirror image rule. Under the mirror image rule, an acceptance must mirror (be the same as) the offer for a contract to exist. When the offeree's acceptance does not mirror the offeror's first offer (Offer 1), then a counteroffer has been created. In the case of a counteroffer (Offer 2), a role reversal occurs, whereby the original offeree (Offeree 1) becomes the new offeror (Offeror 2) relating to the newly created offer in the form of the counteroffer. The original offeror (Offeror 1) now takes on the new role of offeree (Offeree 2) in considering the new offer (Offer 2) by Offeror 2.

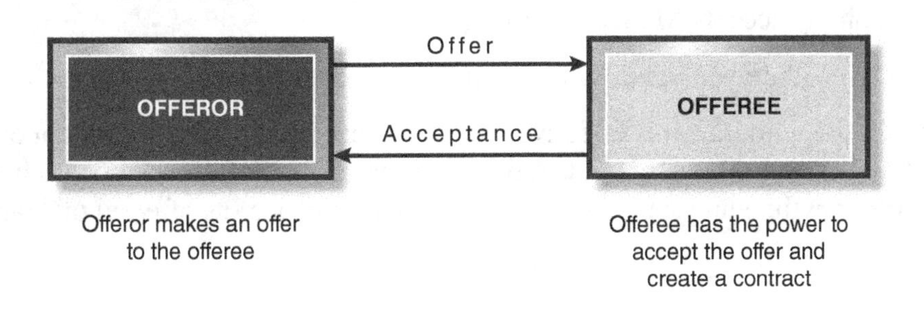

What can invalidate the ability to accept an offer by the offeree? Generally, four events could occur, as follows:

1. Rejection or counteroffer by the offeree
2. Lapse of time (Sometimes a set period of time is written in the agreement, and if not, if a reasonable period of time expires, as determined by the courts.)
3. Revocation of the offer by the offeror
4. Death or incapacity of the offeror or offeree

To reconfirm the American law concepts of offer and acceptance, the next section provides a series of short, hypothetical problem sets. In the following problem sets, only offer and acceptance principles under American contract law are to be applied, separate from the other required contract elements of consideration, legality, and capacity, which are discussed later.

Problem Sets: Offer and Acceptance

The following problem sets involve two hypothetical people, Mariachi and Johnny. The hypothetical events are listed in sequential order. Unless otherwise stated, Mariachi and Johnny's actions should be construed as explicitly manifested to the other party.

1. Assume:
   - Mariachi makes an offer to Johnny.
   - Johnny accepts Mariachi's offer.
   - Mariachi withdraws her offer.

Q1: Is the withdrawal valid? Is there an enforceable contract?

A1: No, the withdrawal is not valid. Yes, an enforceable contract exists, assuming all other elements needed for a validly binding contract exist. Once Johnny accepts Mariachi's offer, a contract is formed. Thereafter, following the contract formation, Mariachi (the offeror) cannot withdraw her offer.

2. Assume:
   - Mariachi makes an offer to Johnny.
   - Mariachi withdraws her offer.
   - Johnny accepts Mariachi's offer.

Q2: Is the withdrawal valid? Is there an enforceable contract?

A2: Yes, the withdrawal is effective. No, an enforceable contract does not exist. Even though Mariachi made the offer, Mariachi (as offeror) can withdraw her offer anytime up to, but before, Johnny's acceptance (as offeree) of Mariachi's offer.

3. Assume:
    - Mariachi makes an offer to Johnny.
    - Mariachi decides to withdraw her offer but does not expressly manifest or otherwise communicate her decision to Johnny.
    - Johnny accepts Mariachi's offer.

Q3: Is the withdrawal effective? Does an enforceable contract exist?

A3: No, the withdrawal is not effective. Yes, an enforceable contract exists, assuming all other elements needed for a validly binding contract exist. Unlike in Problem Set 2, Mariachi only decides to withdraw her offer, but she does not explicitly manifest or communicate her intentions verbally or otherwise to Johnny (the offeree).

4. Assume:
    - Mariachi makes an offer to Johnny, stating to Johnny that her offer is good for only two weeks.
    - Three weeks expire from the time of Mariachi's offer to Johnny.
    - Johnny accepts Mariachi's offer during week three.

Q4: Does an offer exist? Does an enforceable contract exist?

A4: No, an offer does not exist. Thus, Johnny can no longer accept Mariachi's offer, because Mariachi, the offeror, "is the master of [her] offer." As a result, Mariachi (as offeror) is free to set a time limit on her offer of two weeks, after which time the offer no longer exists from an American contract law purview.

5. Assume:
    - Mariachi makes an offer to Johnny, stating that the offer is good for only two weeks.
    - One week passes from the time of Mariachi's offer to Johnny.
    - Mariachi withdraws her offer to Johnny.
    - Johnny accepts Mariachi's offer.

Q5: Is Mariachi's withdrawal valid? Does an enforceable contract exist?

A5: Yes, Mariachi's withdrawal is valid. Mariachi (as offeror) can withdraw her offer at any time before Johnny accepts her offer, which Mariachi did. Thus, generally, because Mariachi's offer was withdrawn, an enforceable contract would be deemed to not exist. However, one exception is if Johnny "relied to his detriment" (known as promissory estoppel or the detrimental reliance principle) on Mariachi's promise, and then Johnny started performing based on the promise. In this case, Johnny may claim recovery damages under promissory estoppel (more on promissory estoppel is discussed in Chapter 4).

6. Assume:
   - Mariachi makes an offer to Johnny.
   - Johnny rejects Mariachi's offer.
   - Johnny then changes his mind, and accepts Mariachi's offer.

Q6: Is Johnny's acceptance valid? Does an enforceable contract exist?

A6: No, Johnny's acceptance is not valid. No, an enforceable contract does not exist. Once Johnny rejects Mariachi's offer, the offer is no longer valid. Applying the objective theory of contracts, no one in Mariachi's position would reasonably believe that Johnny would accept the offer.

7. Assume:
   - Mariachi makes an offer to Johnny to sell a new tablet PC for $10,000.
   - Johnny counteroffers to buy the new tablet PC for $9,000.
   - Johnny then changes his mind, takes back the counteroffer, and accepts the original offer for $10,000.

Q7: Does a contract exist?

A7: No, a contract does not exist. By making a counteroffer, (1) Johnny rejected Marichi's original offer; and (2) Johnny then created a new offer for Mariachi to accept or reject (in this case, the positions are switched, so that Johnny is now the offeror, and Mariachi is now the offeree). As a result, there is no longer an offer that Johnny can accept.

Option Contracts

An option contract is a promise that meets the requirements for the formation of a contract and limits the offeror's power to revoke. These cases are considered offers. A good example of an option contract is a contract related to a land sale or house where the seller allows a specific period of time for the potential land/house buyer to decide whether or not to purchase the property.

An option contract is an irrevocable offer. Thus, a seller cannot decide to not sell the seller's property to the buyer during the designated period of time provided. Also, unlike most contracts that require consideration, option contracts allow for nominal consideration (the concept of consideration is covered in greater detail in Chapter 4).

Here is an example of an option contract:

- A seller wants to sell her land for $100,000.
- A buyer wants to buy the seller's land, but he wants some time to decide whether or not to buy the land.
- The buyer gives the seller $1,000 as consideration in exchange for a one-month hold on the land sale, during which time the seller can only sell her land to the buyer in question.

Contract Remedies

When a contract is formed, what happens when one side breaches the contract? Ultimately, this may come down to the question of deciding what contract remedies exist. For remedies to be provided, the injured party must have suffered some injury attributable to the making of the contractual promise.

Remedies can be broadly grouped into the following categories, among others:

- Expectation damages
- Reliance damages
- Restitutionary damages

Expectation damages restore the promisee (party receiving the promise, also known as the offeree) to the position he would have been in if the promise had occurred as it was originally promised by the promisor (party making the promise). Reliance damages restore the promisee to the position she would have been in if the promise had never been made in the first place. Restitutionary damages restore the "unjust enrichment" gained by the promisor back to the promisee.

Here is an example of a remedies case:

- **Case**: *Sullivan v. O'Connor*, 363 Mass. 579, 296 N.E.2d 183 (1973)
- **Facts**: A female patient asks a plastic surgeon to make her nose look beautiful. The doctor promised to do so, and thus bound himself with an enforceable contract that he would make the patient's nose look beautiful. The nose did not turn out to be beautiful after the surgery.
- **Expectation damages**: Damages = expected nose value – current nose value. The intent is to put the woman in the position she would have been in if the doctor performed as he promised under the contract.
- **Reliance damages**: Damages = original nose value – current nose value. The intent is to put the woman in the position she would have been in if she did not have the surgery.
- **Restitutionary damages**: The intent is to give back to the woman what the doctor "unjustly" received. Because the doctor did not perform what he promised, he unjustly received medical expenses from the woman. Thus, out-of-pocket medical expenses and any other costs that the patient paid to the doctor would be paid back to her as restitutionary damages.

Summary

A validly binding contract requires mutual assent, which can be subdivided into offer and acceptance. The party making the offer is the offeror (promisor). The party deciding to accept or reject the offer is the offeree (promisee). An offer can be revoked up to, but excluding, an acceptance by the offeree. Generally, an advertisement is not an offer. However, exceptions exist in which the advertisement is specific enough to constitute an offer. If the offeree changes the material terms of the offer, the offeree has (1) rejected the offer and (2) created a new offer. Various remedies for a contract breach exist, including expectation damages, reliance damages, and restitutionary damages.

CONTRACTS II
(Consideration and Beyond)

This chapter focuses on the elements needed for a contract above and beyond mutual assent (covered in Chapter 3). Specifically, the initial part of this chapter focuses on the remaining required contract elements of consideration, legality, and capacity. The remaining sections focus on issues that relate to contracts, either directly or indirectly, regarding these four needed contract elements.

Consideration

Consideration is defined as a "bargained-for exchange" of promises and/or acts. Regarding interpretation, consideration has been defined broadly, not narrowly, by American courts. So what qualifies as consideration? Consideration can consist of some right, interest, profit, or benefit accruing to the other party, or some forbearance, detriment, loss, or responsibility given, suffered, or undertaken by the other party. In other words, a promisor does not have to receive a benefit for valid consideration. A waiver of any legal right at the request of the other party to the contract can be sufficient consideration for a promise. Put simply, consideration under American law can be either a benefit or detriment related to the promisor (offeror) and promisee (offeree).

Why is consideration so broad under American law? Various factors exist, but one rationale is the need to allow for flexibility in terms of free market exchange under a "freedom to contract" principle. This principle in effect gives due deference to those involved in the contracts to determine what contract terms and conditions best serve their respective interests. Now that we know that consideration can be interpreted broadly—to include both benefits and detriments to the other parties—the next pertinent question will be discussed.

Must the exchange of consideration, which is needed for a validly binding contract, be "equal"? In other words, does valid consideration exist if inequality in consideration between the contract parties exists? The short answer is generally yes. In the same spirit underlying the freedom to contract principle, inequality of consideration generally can constitute valid consideration, with some exceptions discussed later.

The rationale exists in the following way: Even when inequality of consideration exists, the parties to a contract are free to make a bargain, even if the consideration exchanged is unequal. Under American law, it is enough that something of "real value in the eyes of the law" was exchanged as consideration. Courts will generally not ask whether the thing that forms the consideration is of any substantial value to anyone else besides the parties to the contract. In other words, the determination of value is subjective, in many ways, as seen from the eyes of the parties to the contract. This approach reflects the general notion that it is best for the contractual parties to decide the economics of the transaction (e.g., the exact monetary value of the goods or services being exchanged), not the courts.

Here is an example of inequality of consideration as valid consideration:

- **Facts**: A law school professor gives a copy of her recently published law textbook (retailing for $100) to a student. In exchange, the same student gives the law school professor $50 for the textbook.
- **Issue**: Whether adequacy of valid consideration exists.
- **Rule**: The general rule is that inequality of consideration can constitute valid consideration.
- **Conclusion**: Yes, valid consideration exists (i.e., generally, a $100 retail value law school textbook in exchange for $50 constitutes valid consideration, despite inequality of consideration in terms of fair market value).

Now that we know that consideration can be unequal between the parties, the next question becomes how unequal can consideration be? One exception to this general rule is if the exchange is grossly disproportionate to constitute nominal consideration. In a case involving nominal consideration, in which a disproportionately small consideration amount is given, a risk exists that the courts may not deem the thing exchanged as sufficient valid consideration.

As one example, exchanging a car for a house is not equal in value, but if both parties entered the exchange knowingly, the courts may interpret the exchange to constitute valid consideration. However, exchanging $1 for a $1 million valued home may be construed as nominal consideration, depending on the case circumstances. This is mainly because the transaction resembles more of a "something for nothing" situation than a "something for something" (in Latin, quid pro quo) bargained-for exchange between the parties. Thus, for reasons already discussed, nominal consideration will generally not be deemed as valid consideration under American law.

Can consideration given in the past be valid consideration for a contract in the present or future? The short answer is no. The general rule is that past consideration does not constitute valid consideration under American law. Past consideration is generally interpreted as a benefit or detriment that would form a bargained-for exchange, as discussed earlier. However, past consideration is consideration that has been given before any contract was agreed upon. Thus, past consideration is not deemed sufficient valid consideration to bind a contract.

Here is an example of invalid past consideration:

- **Facts**: A couple has a son. The couple names the child after the mother's grandfather. The grandfather later (following, not at or before, the child's naming) asks the couple to name the child after him (the grandfather's name). In exchange, the grandfather promises to pay for the son's future college expenses. Based on this promise, the couple agrees. The grandfather later revokes his earlier promise.
- **Issue**: Whether the parents can enforce the grandfather's promise.
- **Rule**: The general rule is that past consideration is not valid consideration. Because the couple's naming of the child occurred before the grandfather made the offer, it was past consideration. Thus, the couple cannot bind the grandfather to his (earlier) promise.
- **Conclusion**: No, the parents cannot enforce the grandfather's promise.

Here is an example of valid consideration:

- **Case**: *Hamer v. Sidway*, 124 N.Y. 538, 27 N.E. 256 (1891)
- **Facts**: An uncle promises to pay his nephew $5,000 to not smoke, swear, or gamble until the nephew was 21 years old (assume that all of these acts are legal at the time and jurisdiction of this case). The nephew fully performed on his side. When the nephew turned 21, he wrote to his uncle that he was entitled to the $5,000 per their earlier agreement. The uncle agreed. However, the uncle offered to keep the money for the nephew until the nephew would be ready to receive the money. The nephew agreed. The uncle died soon after, without giving the nephew the $5,000. The nephew made a claim to the executor that was administrating the uncle's assets after his death, Sidway, for the $5,000 plus interest. The nephew's request was rejected by Sidway. The nephew then filed suit.
- **Issue**: Whether giving up smoking, swearing, and gambling is valid consideration?
- **Rule**: The general rule is that consideration for a promise to a contract may consist of, among other things, not just a benefit, but also the abandonment of a legal right.
- **Apply**: Here, the nephew had the legal right to the actions he chose to give up in the form of smoking, swearing, and gambling in exchange for the uncle's promise. Thus, the nephew's forbearance of his legal rights to these acts was sufficient consideration for the promise of $5,000. Applying the general rule, any damage, suspension, or forbearance of a legal right is sufficient to sustain a promise to a contract. As a result, it is sufficient that the nephew in this case restricted his lawful right to smoke, drink, and gamble in exchange for his uncle's promise to pay him $5,000. In other words, generally, a waiver of a legal right

at the request of the counterparty to the contract is sufficient consideration for a promise.

- **Conclusion**: Yes, the giving up of smoking, swearing, and gambling is valid consideration.

The next question becomes whether a promise to provide a gift is an enforceable contract. The short answer is no, gratuitous promises are not enforceable, because a bargained-for exchange of consideration does not exist. This promise is referred to as an unenforceable gratuitous promise. For instance, a promise made by a family member purporting to be a gift is considered a gratuity. Because a gratuity is a gratuitous promise, it is not an enforceable contract. One rationale for this rule of law is that gratuitous promises, or gifts, are generally not intended to be a binding contract.

Consideration for Contract Modifications

As many readers will understand, in an ever-changing legal and economic environment, contracts may need to be modified after contract formation. The question then becomes whether modifying material terms and conditions to a contract require additional consideration for additional changes. The short answer is yes, contract modification to material terms and conditions to a contract generally does require additional consideration.

The rationale for the need for additional consideration to modify a contract exists in the preexisting duty rule, which states that a bargained-for exchange for something that a party is already legally bound to do is not valid consideration. Although promising a preexisting duty is not valid consideration, a similar but not preexisting performance can be deemed as valid consideration, if it differs from what was required by the preexisting duty in a way that reflects more than a pretense of a bargain. In plain English, the new performance must be more than superficially different than the preexisting (performance) duty.

At least one exception to the preexisting duty rule exists: A contract modification may be enforceable even if a preexisting duty existed and no additional consideration was provided, only if all of the following criteria are met:

1. The parties voluntarily agreed to the modification.
2. The promise modifying the original contract was made before the contract was fully performed on either side.
3. The underlying circumstances that prompted the contract modification were unanticipated by the parties.
4. The contract modification is fair and equitable to the parties.

Here is an example of a contract modification:

- **Case**: *Angel v. Murray*, 322 A.2d 630 (R.I. 1974)
- **Facts**: A garbage disposal company and a city made a long-term contract for

the disposal of the city's garbage. A contract modification was made in which the payment by the city to the disposal company was increased, but without additional consideration.

- **Issue**: Whether the contract modification was enforceable, even if no additional consideration was provided to support the increase in payment.
- **Rule**: The general rule is that contract modifications require additional consideration pursuant to the preexisting duty rule. However, an exception to the general rule exists in which no additional consideration is needed for a contract modification, only if all of the aforementioned criteria are met: (1) the parties voluntarily agreed to the modification; (2) the promise modifying the original contract was made before the contract was fully performed on either side; (3) the underlying circumstances that prompted the contract modification were unanticipated by the parties; and (4) the contract modification is fair and equitable to the parties.
- **Apply**: Here, the exception to the general rule existed because (1) the contract modification was made due to unexpected hardships, where the city's population increased rapidly over a short time period, which was unanticipated by both parties; (2) the parties voluntarily agreed to the contract modification; (3) the promise modifying the original contract was made before the contract was fully performed by either party to the contract; and (4) the contract modification was fair and equitable to the parties.
- **Conclusion**: Yes, the contract modification was enforceable, even if no additional consideration was provided to support the increase in payment.

So far, the general requirement for valid consideration of a validly binding contract has been covered, but can an enforceable contract exist without consideration? In other words, does an exception exist to the general rule that valid consideration is needed for a validly binding contract? The short answer is yes, in certain narrow circumstances. One circumstance (and thus, an exception to the general rule requiring valid consideration) exists if the promisee can show detrimental reliance upon the promise made by the promisor. This exception based on detrimental reliance is known as promissory estoppel.

Promissory estoppel is a promise that the promisor should reasonably expect to induce action or forbearance on the part of the promisee (reasonable expectation of reliance) and that actually does induce action or forbearance (in which reasonable expectation of reliance is in fact acted on by the promisee). In these circumstances, the agreement is binding—even if consideration does not exist—if injustice can be avoided with the enforcement of the promise between the promisor and promisee.

Importantly, because the courts understand that a slippery slope can exist—in which an exception to the general rule requiring valid consideration for a binding contract can be overused and even abused—promissory estoppel is not easily awarded by the courts. Still, it is an important exception to know. Moreover, even when American courts utilize promissory estoppel to enforce a contract that may not be enforceable without promissory estoppel, the promise in question is enforced only to the extent that it is necessary to prevent injustice.

Here is an example of promissory estoppel:

- **Case**: *Feinberg v. Pfeiffer Co.*, 22 S.W.2d 163 (1959)
- **Facts**: Feinberg worked for Pfeiffer from the time she (Feinberg) was 17 years old. After many years of working for Pfeiffer, the board adopted a resolution that would increase Feinberg's salary to $400 and create retirement benefits of $200 per month for the rest of her life when she chose to retire. Feinberg continued to work for Pfeiffer for another two years, and then she retired. Pfeiffer promptly began paying Feinberg her retirement benefits on the first day of every month. Pfeiffer's president died in 1949 and was replaced by Pfeiffer's wife, until her son-in-law took over the company in 1953. The son-in-law decided to start sending only $100 per month, rather than $200 per month, beginning on April 1956. Feinberg declined to cash the check and sued based on her argument that a contractual obligation existed to pay her $200 per month in retirement benefits.
- **Issue**: Whether detrimental reliance existed to create an enforceable contract based on promissory estoppel.
- **Rule**: The general rule is that valid consideration is required for an enforceable contract. However, an exception to the general rule exists if detrimental reliance based on promissory estoppel exists.
- **Apply**: Here, the promise to pay Feinberg $200 per month in retirement payment is legally enforceable because (1) Feinberg detrimentally relied on Pfeiffer's promise to pay benefits when she made her decision to retire from Pfeiffer; (2) Pfeiffer's promise to pay Feinberg the additional amount in retirement benefits induced Feinberg to retire (when without inducement, she would have continued to work, based on the court's findings); and (3) injustice can be avoided by enforcing the contract (to pay Feinberg $200 in retirement benefits).
- **Conclusion**: Yes, detrimental reliance existed to create an enforceable contract based on promissory estoppel.

Legality and Capacity

The third element needed for a contract is legality. In other words, the agreement must not violate the public policy and/or any related rules and regulations of the relevant jurisdiction. This element is generally more clear compared to consideration and mutual assent, but it is still useful to provide some examples. For instance, an agreement to buy a car in exchange for $10,000 may likely satisfy the legality element. However, an agreement related to gambling, prostitution, and violent acts against certain persons may likely violate legality in most American jurisdictions.

The fourth element needed for a contract is contractual capacity. In other words, the parties to the contract must be able to understand both the rights (real and/or potential benefits) and responsibilities (real and/or potential risks) of the agreement. Most persons are deemed to have contractual capacity, but certain classes of persons are not, such as minors (under age 18), intoxicated persons, and persons of unsound mind.

Defenses and Exceptions: To Enforcement of a Bargained-for Exchange

Suppose that one of the parties to an agreement believes that a contract has been formed in which all of the elements for a valid contract are met. Assume also that the other party to the agreement wants to dispute the fact that the contract is enforceable. What would be the best legal arguments to support the position that the agreement should not be enforced?

The short answer is that several arguments could be used under American law. Legal arguments exist in the form of defenses and exceptions to the enforcement of a bargained-for exchange. One example is to argue that the agreement is unconscionable (i.e., grossly unfair, in favor of one side). If an agreement is deemed as unconscionable, the court may refuse to enforce the entire agreement, or enforce only the remainder of the contract without the unconscionable provision(s) of the agreement.

Factors considered when deciding on the unconscionability of a contract include the following:

- Community norms and reasonableness
- Quality (overall equality) of the bargaining process
- Use of deceptive or high-pressure techniques or strategies
- Confusing or hidden language in the written agreement

Here is an example of an unconscionable agreement:

- **Case**: *Jones v. Star Credit Co.*, 59 Misc. 2d 189, 298 N.Y.S.2d 264 (1969)
- **Facts**: Plaintiff was a welfare recipient. Defendant was an office represented by a salesperson who visited the plaintiff. Plaintiff purchased a home freezer from the salesperson for $900. After various charges above and beyond the $900 purchase price assessed by the salesperson, the final price for the home freezer was $1,234.80. The retail market price for the home freezer was $300.
- **Issue**: Whether the agreement's terms and conditions were unconscionable, and thus, an unenforceable contract.
- **Rule**: The general rule is that unconscionable (grossly unfair or unequal) agreements are not enforceable contracts. Here, a great price difference existed between the home freezer's retail market price of $300 and the $900 sales price by the

salesperson. Although some price increase is reasonable in a free market economy, a substantial price increase that is multiples of the retail price is "exorbitant on its face." This leads to the belief that the salesperson took advantage of the plaintiff. Moreover, an unequal bargaining power gap clearly existed between the defendant (a lower-income retail customer) and the plaintiff (a large corporation).

- **Conclusion**: Yes, the agreement was unconscionable, thus the remainder of the agreement should no longer be enforced.

Duress is another defense to a contract to argue that the contract should not be enforceable. Duress is formally defined as "any unlawful threat or coercion used . . . to induce another to act (or not act)." More simply, duress is undue pressure placed on a person to coerce that person to perform an act or enter into an agreement that he or she would ordinarily not perform.

Here is an example of duress:

- **Case**: *Alaska Packers' Association v. Domenico*, U.S. Court of Appeals, 9th Circuit, 117 F. 99 (1909)
- **Facts**: On March 26, 1900, the parties entered into a contract under which the plaintiffs/appellees (Domenico) agreed to sail on a ship to Alaska for the 1900 fishing season. After the ship arrived in Alaska, the plaintiffs/appellees stopped working. The workers demanded an increase in their wages, or else they (the workers) would stop working. The ship's superintendent eventually yielded to the workers' demands. However, upon the ship's return, the plaintiff/appellees were informed that they would be paid only the amount originally agreed upon in March, not reflecting the increase in wages, as demanded by the workers after the ship arrived in Alaska.
- **Issue**: Whether the contract modification for workers' wage increases was unenforceable due to duress?
- **Rule**: The general rule is that duress, if proven, is a valid defense to a contract not being enforced. Here, the defendant/appellant's (Alaska Packers' Association) consent to the contract modification for higher worker wages was made under duress. Because contracts, including modification(s) to a contract, under duress are generally not enforceable contracts, the contract modification made under duress is not an enforceable contract.
- **Conclusion**: Yes, the contract modification for workers' wage increases is unenforceable due to duress.

What if the issue in this case related to contract modification/preexisting duty, rather than duress? Would an enforceable contract exist? The short answer is probably yes. In the original version of the case, apart from the fact that the modification was made under duress, no additional consideration was given to make the contract modification enforceable. Also, the ship workers already had a preexisting duty to work. However, if the ship workers promised something additional or new, such as to work more hours or perform extra duties, additional performance promises above and beyond those that already existed under the preexisting duty rule may have been considered as a similar but different promise from the original preexisting promise to constitute additional consideration. Thus, contract modification under these circumstances may have been deemed an enforceable contract under American law.

Illusory promises can also be used in arguing that a contract should not be enforced. Simply put, an illusory promise is a promise with no mutuality of obligation, although it may seem as if bilateral promises exist superficially. In this case, neither party to the agreement involving an illusory promise is bound to his or her promise. This is because an illusory promise gives a "free way out" of the promise, which in effect is not a binding promise needed for a binding contract. So, to stress-test whether a promise is an illusory promise, the issue is whether one or more of the parties to the contract are free to perform, or to withdraw, from the agreement at his or her own discretion. If so, then the promise may likely be deemed as an illusory promise, which is not a form of valid consideration. Thus, with no valid consideration, no valid contract is formed.

Here is an example of an illusory promise:

- **Case**: *Rehm-Zeiher Co. v. F.G. Walker Co.*, 56 Ky. 6, 160 S.W. 777 (Ky. 1913)
- **Facts**: The parties to the contract were in the business of buying and selling whiskey (a type of alcohol). Part of the contract between the parties stated: "If for any unforeseen reason, the party of the second part finds that they cannot use the full amount of the [whiskey], the party of the first part agrees to release them from the contract for the amount desired by the party of the second part."
- **Issue**: Whether the contract (in particular, the contract provision noted above) is an illusory promise, and thus, an unenforceable contract?
- **Rule**: The general rule is that a contract based on an illusory promise is an unenforceable contract. Specifically, in the contract between the parties, no mutuality of obligation exists. Thus, the promise in the contract is an illusory promise. As a result, the contract is not binding because it gives a "free way out" for the parties to the contract.
- **Conclusion**: Yes, an illusory promise exists, and thus, the agreement is an unenforceable contract.

Summary

Contracts are a critical part of our everyday lives. Four elements are needed to form a validly binding legal contract: (1) mutual assent, (2) consideration, (3) legality, and (4) capacity. Consideration is a bargained-for exchange that reflects the need for a quid pro quo (Latin for "something for something"). Consideration can be a benefit and/or a detriment. This means that consideration is defined very broadly and flexibly under American law. However, nominal consideration is normally not considered valid consideration, because it may be interpreted to not be a true bargained-for quid pro quo exchange. Moreover, the agreement must not violate the public policy of the contract's jurisdiction. Finally, the parties to the contract must have contractual capacity. This means the parties must be capable of understanding both the rights and responsibilities of the agreement.

TORTS

Imagine a superstar athlete has a broken foot. The athlete goes to the doctor for help. The doctor promises the athlete a "perfect foot" after surgery. After the consultation meeting with the doctor, the athlete decides to go ahead with the foot surgery. However, after the surgery, the athlete's foot remains in the same condition. So, the foot has not improved and certainly has not met the "perfect foot" standard promised by the doctor. As a result, let's assume that the superstar athlete is no longer able to play competitively within the athlete's professional league for the upcoming season.

The athlete retains you as legal counsel. What type of claim would you seek? The previous chapter covered American contract law, so suing for breach of a contract could be one option. Are there any other options? The short answer is yes. It is possible that a legal claim could also be brought under American tort law. This then begs the question, what exactly is a tort?

To get to an answer for the case scenario, we begin with what a tort is. The term "tort" (meaning "twisted") is a civil wrong, other than a breach of contract, for which the law provides a remedy. The party committing the tort is referred to as the tortfeasor (wrongdoer). The field of tort law is important for a variety of reasons, including that the majority of legal claims in American courts are brought under tort law.

Three types of torts exist as follows:

- Intentional torts (e.g., intentionally hitting a person)
- Negligent torts (e.g., causing an accident by failing to obey traffic rules)
- Strict liability torts (e.g., liability for making and selling defective products)

What then is the difference between the various types of torts? One important difference is the intent underlying each tort. Intentional torts—as the term suggests—require intent to commit the wrongful act. However, negligence and strict liability do not require intent.

Intentional Torts

Intentional tort types include the following:

- Battery
- Assault
- False imprisonment
- Intentional infliction of emotional distress

With torts, and especially intentional torts, what type of burden must be met to support a particular fact or proposition? The answer relates to the concept of establishing a prima facie case. Prima facie is a Latin expression meaning "on its first appearance," or "by first instance." From a litigation strategy perspective, meeting the burden of proof requires the plaintiff to prove that a prima facie case has been established. A prima facie case is a case sufficient on its face that establishes at least the minimum requisite evidence to support a particular proposition or fact.

Battery

In establishing a prima facie case of battery, the plaintiff must prove that (1) the defendant intended to cause a harmful or offensive contact and (2) that contact actually occurred. Thus, the elements for battery (an intentional tort) are (a) intent and (b) harmful or offensive contact.

The concept of intent related to torts was introduced earlier in this section. To go further, intent is often interpreted as the desire to cause the specific result in question. However, courts may infer intent, even when no clear desire to cause a specific result exists. Two concepts are related to inferred intent by the courts. The first type of inferred intent is constructive intent, which is the knowledge or substantial certainty that the result in question will occur. Thus, simply knowing that something may occur and acting in a way so that the result may occur may constitute an intent from the court's perspective. The second type of inferred intent is transferred intent, which allows for a lawsuit by a third party when the tortfeasor X meant to strike Y, but actually ended up hitting a third party Z.

The term "harmful," when used to establish that a battery occurred, can be interpreted as bodily harm in the form of any physical impairment of the condition of another's body, or physical pain or illness. It can also be interpreted to include alterations that may cause harm, such as a doctor improperly removing a wart.

The next step to establish that a battery occurred is to analyze the term "offensive." By what measure do courts determine if an act and/or result was offensive? Generally, an act is considered offensive when it offends a reasonable person's sense of dignity. It may be unwarranted by particular social norms and usages prevalent at the time and place in question. Thus, the interpretation involves yet again another reasonable person standard (covered in Chapter 3). Finally, a contact must occur for battery to be established. This requisite contact can, but does not always have to, be body-to-body physical contact. For example, cigarette smoke may generally not constitute a contact sufficient to establish that a battery occurred (as of this writing). However, cigarette smoke that was intentionally and offensively blown into someone's face by the tortfeasor may constitute battery.

Assault

To establish a prima facie case of assault, the plaintiff must prove that (1) the defendant intended to cause a harmful or offensive contact and (2) the plaintiff was put in imminent apprehension of contact. Thus, the elements to establish a prima facie case of assault are (a) intent, (b) harmful or offensive contact, and (c) imminent apprehension of contact by the plaintiff. One step in determining assault is to analyze the term "imminent." Imminent is interpreted to mean that the apprehension of the contact by the tortfeasor must be within the same moment. However, insults and mere words usually do not constitute assault alone, regardless of how foul or incendiary they may be.

It may appear that battery and assault are very similar in terms of establishing a prima facie case. Do any differences exist? One similarity is that both battery and assault require (a) intentionality or (b) harmful or offensive contact. The difference, however, is whether an actual contact occurred. To establish a prima facie case of assault, the plaintiff must reasonably believe—using a reasonable person standard—that an imminent apprehension of contact existed, but with a prima facie case of battery, actual physical contact must occur.

False Imprisonment

To establish a prima facie case of false imprisonment, the plaintiff must show that (1) the defendant intended to confine the plaintiff; (2) the defendant's acts caused the plaintiff to be confined; and (3) the plaintiff was either conscious of or harmed by the confinement.

Acts "intending to confine" must be within the same moment (simultaneous occurrence must exist). Thus, confining someone the next day does not normally meet this element. At the same time, simple but evocative words, such as "Don't move" or "I'll shoot (you)!" can be interpreted as an act intended to confine if the person is actually confined due to the defendant's words. Furthermore, the confinement must be complete. This means that if a victim has a reasonable way out and is aware of it (e.g., an open door or back exit), then it is generally not actual confinement. However, the person being confined is not required to look for an escape.

Intentional Infliction of Emotional Distress (IIED)

The final example covered in this section regarding intentional torts is intentional infliction of emotional distress (IIED). To establish a prima facie case of IIED, the plaintiff must prove that the defendant acted with outrageous or extreme conduct that recklessly or intentionally caused severe emotional distress to another.

The terms "outrageous or extreme conduct" are words or actions that exceed all standards of decency. In terms of word usage, mere insults or blackmail generally do not meet the standard of being outrageous or extreme. In terms of physical acts, acts of possible but not actual violence (e.g., raising a fist or weapon) generally do not meet the standard of being outrageous or extreme. For example, throwing a dead body in someone's front yard or delivery of the wrong body by a funeral home have been ruled to not constitute outrageous or extreme conduct.

So far in this chapter, the elements needed by the plaintiff in a tort case have been covered. The next section takes the opposite viewpoint in terms of explaining affirmative defenses that can be used when faced with tort action causes of action.

Affirmative Defenses

An affirmative defense is made after the plaintiff successfully proves a prima facie case for an intentional tort. At this point, the burden of proof then shifts from the plaintiff to the defendant. An affirmative defense is also known as a "privilege."

Affirmative defenses include the following:

- Consent
- Necessity
- Self-defense
- Defense of others
- Defense of property

Consent

Consent is the willingness in fact for the conduct to occur. Thus, even if the plaintiff proves a prima facie case, the defendant can argue that the plaintiff consented to the act. Consent can be communicated directly to the defendant, but it does not always have to be communicated to the defendant. In the latter case, the defendant can argue that implied consent existed.

Here is an example of implied consent:

- **Case**: *O'Brien v. Cunard Steamship*, 154 Mass. 272, 28 N.E. 266 (1891)
- **Facts**: A woman sued a boat company for battery related to the boat company's action of injecting her with a medical vaccination. However, the facts show that she was not forced to take the medical vaccination (i.e., it was optional, not obligatory).
- **Issue**: Whether implied consent existed, and whether a tortious act was committed.
- **Rule**: The general rule is that consent can exist in the form of implied consent.
- **Apply**: The court decided that the woman (plaintiff), while knowing that she

would be vaccinated, raised her arm to receive the vaccination. Thus, the plaintiff's voluntary physical raising of her arm to receive the vaccination was a form of implied consent to receive the vaccination. Thus, even if she proved a prima facie case of battery, the defendant had a valid affirmative defense in the form of implied consent to the vaccination.

- **Conclusion**: Yes, implied consent existed, thus no tortious act was committed.

Another subset of consent within affirmative defenses is the concept of emergency consent. An affirmative defense of emergency consent is acknowledged if (1) the plaintiff was unable to consider the matter; (2) an immediate decision was necessary; (3) no reason existed for the plaintiff to object to the emergency consent; and (4) a reasonable person would not have objected to the emergency consent.

Furthermore, much like a sports game of litigation volleyball, defenses to the affirmative defense of consent exist. Specifically, examples of defenses to consent include (1) coercion (in providing consent), (2) distress, and (3) fraud. As a result, even if the defendant proves that consent was given, consent generally cannot normally be deemed a proper defense if it was coerced or given under distress or fraud. For instance, in the previous case example involving implied consent, if the woman (plaintiff) provided evidence that she was coerced by the doctor (or other staff), then the court may have upheld the decision for the plaintiff by ruling that no consent, including implied consent, was given by the plaintiff.

Consent is generally deemed as not a proper defense when it is given under the following circumstances: (1) lack of capacity to consent (e.g., consent by minors under 18 years of age); (2) lack of mental capacity (e.g., intoxicated persons); and (3) consent to a criminal act (e.g., slavery or indentured servitude).

Necessity

Necessity exists when the defendant is privileged (legally allowed) to enter or remain on another's land, which would normally be deemed as trespassing, or allowed to trespass to the chattel of another, if it is, or reasonably appears to be, necessary to prevent serious harm. For example, assume a situation where a defendant was sued for throwing away the plaintiff's barrel of wine on a ferry boat in an attempt to save the boat and its passengers amid a storm. Could the defendant argue that necessity existed?

In a case with such facts, based on the famous Mouse Case (12 Co. 63 (1608)), the court held that, yes, the privilege of necessity did exist. The court's rationale was that the defendant's acts were necessary for the defendant to throw away the barrel of wine to prevent serious harm (e.g., saving the boat from sinking and its passengers from drowning). Moreover, the barrel of wine would have been lost anyway if the boat sank.

Self-Defense

In deciding whether to grant self-defense, American courts will consider the forces used by the plaintiff (as the alleged attacker) and the defendant (as the alleged victim).

It is important that the victim uses reasonable force that is deemed appropriate in the situation. Thus, if A tried to hit B, and B kills A in response, B's act cannot constitute self-defense, because it would not be deemed as "reasonable force."

What then is the difference between nondeadly force and deadly force? Distinguishing between the two types of force is often needed when deciding on the reasonableness of the force used by the alleged victim (defendant). In plain English, deadly force can cause death or serious bodily harm. Everything else can generally default to nondeadly force.

A person can generally use deadly force as self-defense only when a reasonable belief exists that the tortfeasor is about to intentionally inflict death or serious bodily harm that can be prevented only by the immediate use of force, and the person is either within his or her household or has nowhere to retreat. A person can generally use nondeadly force as self-defense only when a reasonable belief exists that the other party will intentionally inflict unprivileged harm to him or her. Much like with the other defenses, nondeadly force must be reasonable.

Defense of Others

Here, the defense of others varies greatly from state to state. The majority view is that the defendant has a privilege to defend another person only if that person had the privilege of self-defense. If the defendant was mistaken about the need to defend, then no privilege exists. Thus, if A points a water gun at B, and C thinks that B is in danger and shoots A with a real gun, C is not privileged. The minority view is that the defendant is privileged to defend another if the defendant reasonably believes that the other would be privileged to defend him or herself if able to do so. Even if mistaken, the defendant might still have the privilege if the belief was deemed as reasonable. Thus, in the previous water gun case under the minority view, C may be privileged if he reasonably believed that A was about to shoot B with a real gun.

In terms of distinguishing between deadly and nondeadly force, the same methodology as used with self-defense is used, and similarly, the force used must be reasonable.

Defense of Property

The final affirmative defense covered in this section is the defense of property. A person can use deadly force as a defense of property only when he or she reasonably believes that an intruder, unless forced out, is likely to cause death or serious bodily harm. A person can use nondeadly force as a defense of property only when (1) the intrusion was not privileged; (2) the defendant reasonably believed that the intrusion could only be prevented by force; and (3) the defendant first requested the intruder to desist, or the defendant reasonably believed that a request would be useless even if stated to the intruder.

Res Ipsa Loquitur

How do you prove a tort case without direct evidence? One legal strategy would be to apply res ipsa loquitor, which is used when the plaintiff does not have direct evidence of the act that caused injury. This concept is often employed by the plaintiff's legal counsel when direct evidence is missing or incomplete. For instance, imagine walking down the street in New York City. You are then hit by a large and heavy bucket filled with paint from somewhere above you in the building next to you. After a long search, you believe you find the tortfeasor, but you do not have direct evidence to prove the person's negligent behavior.

With res ipsa loquitor, even if the plaintiff cannot identify exactly what the defendant did in being negligent, the plaintiff is not necessarily precluded from recovering legal damages where negligence is apparent. To prove res ipsa loquitur, the plaintiff must demonstrate that (1) generally, the accident would not have occurred but for the defendant's negligence; and (2) the cause of harm was in the defendant's exclusive control.

As another example, one case involving res ipsa loquitur involved a waitress who had a Coca-Cola bottle burst while she held it in her hands, causing her physical injury. The waitress-plaintiff used res ipsa loquitur to argue that the defendant's (Coca-Cola) negligence caused her hand injury. The waitress-plaintiff used res ipsa loquitur and demonstrated that (1) the bottle no longer existed; and (2) she could not provide any actual evidence of negligence by the defendant, because the defendant had exclusive control over the manufacturing process of the Coca-Cola bottles (based on *Escola v. Coca-Cola Bottling Co.*, 24 Cal. 2d 453 (1944)).

Causation

To decide whether negligence existed, American courts generally use the "but for" causation test. For example, if A violated a traffic law and B died because of a heart attack in another country, A is not liable for B's death because A's acts (even if negligent) did not directly cause B's death. Applying the "but for" causation test, the issue is whether A's negligent act was the "but for cause" of B's death, or would B have died "but for" (as a result of) A's negligence?" The short answer is no. The rationale is that B would have died regardless of A's negligent acts. Thus, A is not the "but for cause" of B's death, so A is not liable for B's death.

A separate but related causation test used by American courts is the proximate cause test. Even if A's act is deemed the "but for" cause for B's injury, a court can subsequently apply the proximate cause test, often to ensure that the damages awarded are fair and not overly disproportionate to the injury caused. The determination of proximate cause is a question for the jury (i.e., it is a question of fact for the jury in a jury trial, rather than a question of law for the judge). In a jury trial, the jury's role is to decide whether the defendant's negligence was a cause close enough to have injured the plaintiff. Thus, another informal way to think about proximate cause is the "close enough" cause. In doing so, the jury often considers whether the injury was reasonably foreseeable or not.

Here is an example of "but for" and proximate cause:

- **Facts**: A hits B in a traffic accident. It is clear that A hit B after violating a traffic law.

- **Issue**: Whether A's act was negligent under the "but for" and proximate cause test.
- **Rule**: The general rule is that A's act must be deemed the "but for" and proximate cause of B's injury to determine if A's act was negligent.
- **Apply**: Here, A's act was the "but for" cause, and A's act was a proximate cause of B's injury.
- **Conclusion**: Yes, A was negligent.

Here is another example of proximate cause:

- **Facts**: A hits a tree with his car. The tree then falls on top of a dog, which starts barking. The barking dog alarms a nearby cat, which bites B. The cat bite injures B.
- **Issue**: Whether A is negligently liable for B's injury?
- **Rule**: The general rule is that A's act must be the proximate cause of B's injury to be negligently liable.
- **Apply**: Here, the events between A's act of hitting a tree and B's injury by the cat bite are too remote and not reasonably foreseeable.
- **Conclusion**: No, A is not negligently liable for B's injury.

Injury

The previous hypotheticals involved acts leading to injury. Broadly speaking, many people may think that they know what an injury is, such as physical injury or harm. But would emotional harm constitute an injury? What about economic harm? The short answer is that both emotional and economic harm can be considered an injury in certain cases.

The two main types of nonphysical injury cases are the following:

- Negligent Infliction of Emotional Distress (NIED)
- Negligent Infliction of Economic Harm (NIEH)

Negligent Infliction of Emotional Distress (NIED)

NIED is considered when mental or emotional distress exists as a result of the defendant's negligence, but without any physical injury. Imagine a case where a child is hit by a car. The child's family would go through a great deal of emotional distress. Thus, the issue of NIED is whether the family can receive remedies for emotional harm.

Negligent Infliction of Economic Harm (NIEH)

A defendant is negligent under NIEH when she causes both physical and economic harm to a plaintiff. Under NIEH, physical harm includes both injury to a person or to her property. However, the general rule is that the plaintiff must suffer physical harm in addition to economic harm to recover damages. Without physical harm, economic damages cannot be recovered under NIEH, which has been considered as arguably too strict by some commentators and courts due to the physical harm element requirement.

Employer-Employee Relationships (Applying Vicarious Liability)

Strict liability is liability without fault. (Strict liability not involving vicarious liability will be discussed again later in this chapter.) With strict liability, intent is a nonissue. If the act was committed, regardless of the defendant's intent, liability is established.

Vicarious liability—also known as respondent superior—is a form of strict liability. Many cases involving vicarious liability relate to employer-employee liability issues. For instance, an employer may be vicariously liable for harm caused by an employee where the employee is negligent, but the employer is not liable.

The policy rationale for vicarious liability is to (1) make businesses internalize the cost of safety and (2) encourage businesses to run more safely and efficiently. In vicarious liability cases, the defendant (employer) can recover damages from the employee who was deemed negligent through a legal process known as indemnification.

Under vicarious liability, to hold an employer vicariously liable, the person who committed the negligent act must have been an employee of the company. Thus, the issue would be how to determine whether the particular person was an "employee" of the company or not. To get to an answer, a master-servant relationship test can be applied. The first question would be if the person was a servant or an independent contractor. Employers are generally only liable for the acts of their servant-type employees, and not independent contractors. As one threshold stress-test, the higher the degree of control the employer has over the particular person, the more likely the courts will determine that the particular person is an employee of the employer.

The next question would be, "Assuming the person is an employee of the employer, was the employee acting 'within the scope of employment' during the tortious (wrongful) act?" This question related to the scope of the employee's employment is decided by the judge or jury. Generally, the acts that were carried out while furthering the business of the employer are often considered as acting within the scope of employment.

If, however, a servant-type employee decides to "frolic and detour" from his normal scope of employment, then courts generally construe these actions as not within the scope of his employment. For example, an employee committing a tortious act during lunchtime at his personal home would generally be considered a "frolic and detour," and thus, acting outside of the scope of his employment.

As mentioned in this section, the general rule is that employers are not liable for the negligent acts of independent contractors. However, exceptions exist when the employer does the following, as decided by the judge or jury:

- Was negligent in supervising the independent contractor
- Required the independent contractor to do an inherently dangerous activity
- Gave an independent contractor a nondelegable duty

Duty to Rescue

Imagine that you are relaxing next to a beautiful swimming pool. You then notice a baby crawling toward the swimming pool. If you do nothing, the baby will likely fall into the swimming pool and then drown. No one else is nearby. Does a duty to rescue the baby exist?

Our moral or emotional side may tell us that surely we should help by trying to save the baby from drowning, but under American common law, which gives the freedom to states to pass state laws to the contrary, no duty to rescue generally exists. Thus, even if you see the baby will be in great danger, no duty to rescue the baby would exist under common law. This general rule also applies to medical professionals, which may be surprising to many people. Thus, for instance, medical doctors who are not under a contractual duty otherwise have no duty to rescue.

Exceptions exist, however, in which a duty to rescue prevails. If a person falls under an exception, in which a duty to rescue does exist, then the person's inaction or failure to rescue would be deemed as a negligent act under tort law. Under three jurisdictions—Michigan, Rhode Island, and Vermont—a duty to rescue exists (at the time of this writing). Moreover, when a person begins to rescue, he or she must complete the action (i.e., the rescue cannot be done halfway).

The majority of U.S. states have adopted versions of the Good Samaritan law, which protects the rescuer from negligence liability that may occur during the rescue, in a case where an individual attempts to rescue a person although no legal duty exists to do so. Another exception exists when the victim reasonably relied on the rescuer, but the rescuer did not end up performing the rescue. For example, if A was in a car accident and B told A, "I'll be back with help to rescue you!" but never returns, then B may be liable for A's injury. Another exception is when A creates the need to be rescued. For example, if B were the driver of the car that A was the passenger in when A was injured, and B was not injured, then B would generally have a duty to rescue A under Good Samaritan laws.

Landowner Liability

What are the duties when entering property, as either a landowner or the person entering the premises? This section provides a general legal landscape for thinking about and getting to the answers regarding such issues under American law.

Trespasser

A trespasser is defined as a person who enters another's property without the privilege to do so, assuming no owner consent was given (2nd Restatement of Torts). Generally, a landowner does not owe a duty to unforeseen trespassers, although exceptions can exist.

There are different types of trespassers. Constant trespassers are those who are (1) constantly on an owner's land as a trespasser to land and (2) someone the landowner knows or should know who constantly trespasses on a limited area of the owner's land. For example, let's say a path exists on A's land, and B has been using this path for the past 20 years. B would thus be a constant trespasser, because she meets the constant trespasser criteria: (1) B has been constant on the land; and (2) A knows or should have known that B was constantly on the owner's land.

In the case of constant trespassers, liability for the landowner occurs when each of the following exists:

- An artificial condition is created by the landowner (an artificial condition is any condition that is not natural). Thus, anything created by the landowner would generally be deemed an artificial condition by the courts.
- The landowner knows or has reason to know of the constant trespasser.
- The artificial condition may cause death or serious injury.
- The landowner has reason to believe that the trespasser will not discover the artificial condition.
- The landowner has not exercised reasonable care to warn the trespasser of the artificial condition and the risk involved.

Another type of trespasser is a known trespasser. A known trespasser is a trespasser who is not a constant trespasser, but who is seen by the landowner.

In the case of known trespassers, liability for the landowner occurs when each of the following exists:

- An artificial condition is maintained by the landowner.
- The artificial condition involves a risk of death or serious bodily harm.
- The landowner knows or has reason to know of the trespasser's presence in dangerous proximity to the artificial condition.
- The known trespasser will likely not discover the risk.
- The landowner fails to exercise reasonable care to warn the known trespasser.

American tort law has also created a separate duty for children regarding landowner liability, referred to as the attractive nuisance doctrine (also known as the turntable doctrine).

In the case of attractive nuisance, liability for the landowner exists when each of the following arise:

- An artificial condition exists on the land.
- The child is too young to appreciate the danger of the artificial condition.
- The landowner knows or has reason to know that the child is likely to trespass on her land.
- The landowner realizes or should realize that an unreasonable risk of death or serious bodily harm exists to children.
- The utility of maintaining the artificial condition and burden of eliminating the danger are slight compared to the risk to the child.
- The landowner failed to use reasonable care to eliminate the danger or to protect the child (or children).

One example of applying the attractive nuisance doctrine involves a swimming pool, which is a type of artificial condition under American tort law. Landowners are at times liable for not exercising reasonable care or eliminating the risk of the danger posed by the swimming pool.

Invitee

Separate from these types of trespassers is the concept of an invitee entering a landowner's property. An invitee is a person whom the landowner invited (consented) to enter the landowner's premises. An invitee includes members of the public, business visitors, and employees, to name a few. For invitees, the landowner has a duty to protect invitees from all unreasonable risks.

In the case of invitees, liability for the landowner exists when each of the following exists:

- The landowner knew or should have known that a condition involved an unreasonable risk of harm to the invitee.
- The landowner should have expected the invitee to not discover or realize the danger or to fail to protect him or herself against the danger.
- The landowner failed to exercise reasonable care to protect the invitee against danger.

Licensee

Another type of invited person onto a landowner's premises is a licensee. A licensee is a person who has permission (landowner consent) to enter the landowner's premises, but only for particular purposes (e.g., as a social guest). For licensees, a landowner has a duty to warn of known dangerous conditions and does not have a duty to protect licensees from all unreasonable risks.

Strict Liability

Strict liability represents the strictest type of duty in torts. Strict liability is a legal doctrine that makes a person liable for damages and loss suffered by his or her acts and omissions, regardless of culpability. Strict liability applies not only in torts (e.g., product liability cases) but also in criminal law (covered in Chapter 7).

What elements are needed for strict liability? The plaintiff needs only to prove that the tort actually happened and that the defendant was responsible for the act. Neither good faith nor the fact that the defendant took all possible care and precaution to prevent the harm or suffering is a valid defense under strict liability (hence the term strict liability). For this reason, strict liability is sometimes called absolute liability.

When does strict liability apply? The earlier paragraph noted that strict liability can apply to product liability cases, and further, it is also often used in cases involving the handling of hazardous or inherently dangerous activities. A classic law school example of this involves the owner of a tiger rehabilitation center. No matter how strong the tiger cages are, if the tiger improbably escapes and causes damage and injury to others, then the tiger owner will generally be held liable under strict liability. Another example is a contractor hiring a demolition subcontractor that lacks proper insurance for doing the job. If the demolition subcontractor makes a mistake, then the contractor is generally strictly liable for any damages that occur as a result.

Given the severity of strict liability, what would be the policy rationale for it? First, it discourages reckless behavior and needless loss by forcing potential defendants to take every possible precaution to avoid possible harm. Second, strict liability simplifies litigation and allows the victim to "become whole" more quickly (i.e., puts back the plaintiff to the position he or she would have been in if the wrongful act had not occurred).

Damages

Two main types of tort damages exist. The first type is compensatory (actual) damages, which relate directly to the tortious act. The second type is punitive (exemplary) damages, which are awarded above and beyond compensatory damages as a clear disapproval of the tortious acts committed in the present case and as a disincentive for future potential tortious acts.

Summary

Torts is a noncriminal, noncontract field of civil law. Most lawsuits in the American legal system relate directly or indirectly to tort law in terms of the number of cases filed. Thus, it is an important area of American law, given its sheer prevalence within the American judicial system. Tort types include intentional torts, negligent torts, and strict liability torts.

Examples of intentional torts include assault and battery. Affirmative defenses can be used in the event that tort actions are raised. Affirmative defenses include consent to the acts, necessity for the acts, self-defense, defense of others, and defense of property. Legal concepts such as res ipsa loquitur, "but for" causation, and proximate causation relate to proving negligence in a court of law.

Regarding whether negligence led to injury, American courts can take a relatively expansive view in terms of what constitutes an injury. Physical harm, emotional harm (under Negligent Inflection of Emotional Distress, or NIED), and economic harm (under Negligent Infliction of Economic Harm, or NIEH) may qualify as injury in certain cases.

Employers also have certain potential liability under vicarious liability (a form of strict liability), while landowners also can have certain potential liability and duties to both trespassers and nontrespassers. Finally, in terms of liability, strict liability is the most severe type of liability imposed under American tort law, often used in product liability cases, as well as cases involving hazardous or inherently dangerous activities.

CONSTITUTIONAL LAW

Constitutional law has some of the most controversial issues embedded in it. Abortion, affirmative action, freedom of speech, impeachment, and the power to levy taxes are just some examples of potentially polarizing issues underlying constitutional law. The Constitution underlying constitutional law also provides the foundational framework for American law, which this chapter discusses. For these reasons, constitutional law is of critical importance in understanding the basic tenets underlying American law.

The U.S. Constitution: A Brief History

The U.S. Constitution was created in 1787. Originally, it was composed of seven main articles. Later, in 1791, a Bill of Rights, along with 17 subsequent amendments, culminated into what we know as the U.S. Constitution today. In total, the Constitution is a fairly short written document, containing approximately 4,400 words. This is noteworthy, given its power and influence today and throughout the nation's history. (See Appendix B for the full written texts of the U.S. Constitution and the Bill of Rights.)

The Constitution includes in it the following areas:

- Creates the structure and function of the government
- Defines the relationship between individuals and the government
- Defines and clarifies the powers of the government at the national and state level, as well as the interaction and power hierarchy between the two
- Prohibits the government from taking certain actions

Constitutional law relates to issues such as the following:

- What is the extent of individual freedoms?
- What if one branch of government acts unconstitutionally?
- How much government intrusion into individual lives is constitutional?
- How do the courts determine whether a law is constitutional?

Constitutional Interpretation

How do American courts determine whether a law is constitutional? Clearly, everyone is reading the same written text—the U.S. Constitution—but the critical issue is not what is written, but how to interpret what was written in the Constitution. Two approaches exist relating to constitutional interpretation: (1) originalism and (2) nonoriginalism.

Under the originalism approach, the view is that the Constitution should be narrowly interpreted according to the intent of the original framers of the Constitution (the Framers) or the understanding of the Constitution's provisions at the time of its adoption in the late 18th century. One rationale for this approach is to preserve the Constitution by not altering its interpretation to fit modern society's current environment.

With the originalism approach, certain questions arise. How do courts know what the Framers would think about a particular issue in the 21st century (e.g., cyberissues, drones)? Even assuming a court today can somehow step into the shoes of the original Framers, would this always be the most appropriate approach to take, given how society has changed since the Constitution's creation? Originalists would likely counterargue that the basic tenets underlying the Framers' intent still provide the necessary foundational framework to resolve issues today, and that understanding historical events helps us to understand and shape current and future events.

The second constitutional interpretation approach is nonoriginalism. Under the nonoriginalism approach, the view is that the courts must look beyond the intent of the Constitutional Framers or the understanding of the Constitution's provisions at the time of its adoption in the late 18th century. One rationale for this approach is to adopt the Constitution to fit modern society's current environment. In doing so, courts often look not only to the Constitution's text, but also at history, past precedent cases, dictum in relevant cases, as well as modern-day socioeconomic and political realities.

So far, the concepts underlying the Constitution and the courts' ability to interpret the Constitution have been discussed. But to take a slight step back, one issue that is examined, particularly in U.S. law schools, is where in the Constitution the courts—specifically, the U.S. Supreme Court—were given the power of judicial review to determine whether a law or act is constitutional?

The short answer is that the U.S. Supreme Court was originally not directly given power of judicial review under the Constitution. Instead, it was given this authority through a seminal and landmark series of cases, first and foremost, in a case known as *Marbury v. Madison* (1803).

The Supreme Court's Authority to Interpret the Constitution

Article III of the Constitution relates to the judicial branch, while Article I deals with the legislative branch and Article II deals with the executive branch. Article III states that "[t]he Judicial Power of the United States shall be vested in one Supreme Court, and in such inferior Courts as the Congress may from time to time ordain and establish." Thus, Article III merely allows for the creation of one Supreme Court and "inferior Courts," but whether the Supreme Court had the authority to be the final arbiter on issues of constitutionality was unclear at the Constitution's inception.

Many people are surprised at how little attention Article III received from the Framers compared to Articles I and II. Article III grants the Supreme Court original jurisdiction (i.e., jurisdiction in the first instance, rather than through appeal) in cases related to foreign diplomats or state parties, but not beyond the scope of these cases unless it is through a judicial appeal from a lower court.

In *Marbury v. Madison*, Marbury sued Madison under the Judiciary Act of 1789, which was passed by the legislative branch. Under the Judiciary Act of 1789, the Supreme Court's original jurisdiction was expanded beyond its original mandate by Congress to include the power to issue writs of mandamus (a court order to a lower tribunal to perform or not perform a designated act) against federal officials. In its ruling, Chief Justice Marshall of the Supreme Court ruled that the Supreme Court did not have the additional legal authority under the Constitution—expressly granted under the Judiciary Act of 1789—to compel the delivery of a specified commission (the delivery of the commission by Madison, the new Secretary of State, was a needed documentary process for Marbury to become a Justice). In an interesting plot twist, the previous Secretary of State was Marshall, the current Supreme Court Chief Justice deciding the *Marbury v. Madison* case.

What makes this case so noteworthy and precedent setting is the rationale underlying why Chief Justice Marshall ruled that his court did not have proper legal authority. In a sense, Chief Justice Marshall's ruling represented a very strategic and deliberate move to expand the power of his presiding court, the Supreme Court, in a unique way. Specifically, Chief Justice Marshall argued that the Judiciary Act of 1789 had unconstitutionally expanded the powers of the Supreme Court's original jurisdiction beyond those limited powers expressly granted under Article III of the Constitution. Thus, according to the Supreme Court's landmark ruling in 1803, it did not have jurisdiction to hear the case.

The slight irony and strategy by Chief Justice Marshall in the case was that by declining a relatively smaller amount of greater power (originally given under the Judiciary Act of 1789), the court gained far greater power through judicial review of all constitutional issues, by appointing itself as the final authority as to whether the Judiciary Act of 1789, or any other act, was constitutional or not. Thus, through the Supreme Court's landmark ruling, it was established that Congress was prohibited from establishing any law contrary to the U.S. Constitution, and that it is the role of the Judicial branch to determine what is or is not constitutional. The Supreme Court did not expressly have such legal authority prior to *Marbury v. Madison*.

Supreme Court's Authority to Review State Court Cases

Article III of the Constitution, as stated earlier, originally did not expressly grant the Supreme Court the power of judicial review over state courts, similar to how Article III did not expressly grant the power of review to the Supreme Court initially. However, over several cases within the early years of the court system, we now have a judiciary branch in which it is clear that the Supreme Court has firmly asserted its power of review over state-level, nonfederal court cases, in addition to federal issues, as was established under *Marbury v. Madison.*

One of the first seminal cases relates to a case called *Martin v. Hunter's Lessee.* In the case, the Supreme Court ruled that the interpretation of a treaty was relevant to a land dispute in the state of Virginia. The Supreme Court then remanded the case back to the Virginia Supreme Court. However, and provocatively (in today's terms), the Virginia Supreme Court argued that the U.S. Supreme Court did not have the power of review over cases that began in state courts. Yet again, the U.S. Supreme Court was being tested in its early years, this time at the state level. Ultimately, the U.S. Supreme Court concluded the controversy by ruling to reverse the state court's decision on appeal. In doing so, the U.S. Supreme Court ruled that federal law issues (here, treaty law) initially considered at the state level were within the U.S. Supreme Court's jurisdiction. Thus, America's highest court established its own supremacy over state courts, as well as federal courts, regarding constitutional interpretation on civil law matters.

Cohens v. Virginia expanded the U.S. Supreme Court's power of review one step further by establishing its supremacy over state courts regarding constitutional interpretation on criminal law matters. In the case, the Cohens were prosecuted by the state of Virginia for selling lottery tickets from Washington, D.C. (a federal territory, not a U.S. state) in Virginia, violating Virginia state criminal law. State authorities tried and convicted the Cohens. The same state authorities, provocatively (in today's terms) also declared that their decision was the final decision related to disputes involving states and the federal government. On appeal, the U.S. Supreme Court upheld the convictions. In doing so, the U.S. Supreme Court asserted itself with full appellate power of review and jurisdiction over both civil and now criminal cases at the state court level.

The Supreme Court's widening jurisdiction was made possible because of the Supremacy Clause under Article VI, Section 2 of the Constitution: "The Constitution, and the Laws of the United States . . . shall be the supreme Law of the Land, and the Judges in every State shall be bound thereby." However, the Supremacy Clause does not expressly say whether the Constitution is supreme (a higher legal authority) relative to the "law of the land" at the federal or state level. It also did not state whether the Supreme Court had the power of review acting as the final authority regarding whether a particular issues was or was not constitutional, which, as previously covered, began to be established with a series of landmark cases, including *Marbury v. Madison.*

What powers do states have today under the Constitution? State power is granted under general authority, which is the case because the Constitution does not explicitly specify what powers the states have. Viewed another way, the states have the authority remaining outside the explicit (limited) enumerated powers granted to the federal government under the Constitution. The Tenth Amendment in the Bill of Rights states: "The powers not delegated to the United States by the Constitution, nor prohibited by it to the States, are reserved to the States respectively, or to the people."

What Authority Does the Constitution Give to the Federal Government?

The federal government was founded on a government of limited authority. Specifically, the federal government only has express enumerated powers granted to it under the Constitution. From a big-picture purview, the states have independent constitutional status and general police powers, while the federal government only has expressly enumerated powers.

Other safeguards exist to ensure that the Constitution would not be violated, such as the system of checks and balances and separation of powers, whereby one branch of government has certain authority to ensure that other branches of the federal government are not abused and are acting in conformity with the Constitution. Yet another safeguard against abuse of power by an overreaching government is through specific guarantees adopted in 1791, known as the Bill of Rights.

Executive Powers under Article II of the Constitution

Article II of the Constitution defines the powers of the executive branch. In it, the U.S. President has specific powers, including, among other things:

- Acting as Commander in Chief of the armed forces
- Entering into treaties
- Appointing ambassadors, judges, and executive officials

The U.S. President's powers may seem somewhat limited on paper, especially given many people's perception that the American president is the most powerful person in the world. However, the Constitution and subsequent U.S. Supreme Court case law suggests that the President has all the powers that would normally be associated with the office, even if these powers are not expressly enumerated under the Constitution. At the same time, the President's powers, as part of the executive branch, are under a system of checks and balances by the judicial and legislative branches. Specifically, the judicial branch could, for example, rule that an act by the President was unconstitutional, and the legislative branch could enact impeachment proceedings against the President for an alleged violation of the President's duties under the Constitution.

Summary

The U.S. Constitution represents the highest source of law under American law. High-profile and often controversial topics, such as abortion, affirmative action, equal protection, and freedom of speech, fall under the ambit of constitutional law. The power of review by the Supreme Court was not expressly stated under the Constitution, but soon after the Constitution's adoption, a series of landmark cases arose, which clarified and asserted the U.S. Supreme Court's authority to be the final arbiter in cases relating to whether or not an act is constitutional.

CRIMINAL LAW AND PROCEDURE

When many people envision lawyers, often the image that appears is of a tense criminal law court scene from a famous TV show or movie. In the image is a young, attractive, and highly articulate lawyer seeking justice in front of a packed and attentive courtroom listening to the lawyer's every word.

Relating to criminal cases—and to distinguish fact from fiction in these scenes—this chapter focuses on the field of criminal law and procedure. Criminal law can be divided into substantive and procedural aspects of criminal law. Criminal law overviews and defines what behavior is criminal behavior, along with the general principles underlying criminal liability for criminal behavior. Criminal procedure is defined as the process by which criminal behavior is adjudicated. This chapter's initial section focuses on criminal law, subsequently followed by criminal procedure.

Criminal Law

Criminal law's main issues include the following:

- Whether the defendant committed a criminal act (in Latin, actus reas, meaning the defendant's "physical act").
- Whether the defendant performed the criminal act with the requisite culpable state of mind (in Latin, mens rea, meaning the criminal defendant's "mental state").
- Whether any criminal defenses exist for the defendant (assuming the defendant performed the criminal act with the requisite culpable state of mind).

Criminal Mental States

Definitions of criminal offenses have traditionally varied from state to state, causing potential confusion. The Model Penal Code (MPC) sought to clarify potential confusion by creating four definitions of mental states, as follows:

1. **Purposely**: The mental state when a "conscious object to engage in conduct of that nature or to cause such a result" exists. So, if A kills B because A's intent was to kill B, then A killed B purposely under the MPC.
2. **Knowingly**: Occurs when an act that is "practically certain" that A's conduct will cause an outcome that is a criminal act, or that A is aware of the nature or circumstances of A's conduct.
3. **Recklessly**: Exists when A "consciously disregards a substantial and unjustifiable risk."
4. **Negligently**: Occurs when A should have been aware of a risk, but was careless (negligent), so that A was not aware of the risk.

Criminal Defenses

What types of criminal defenses exist? Generally, two types exist: (1) justification and (2) excuses. Justification includes (a) self-defense, (b) acting under official authority, and (c) other circumstances that involve a "least worst" choice. The need for self-defense can be tested by asking, "Did the defendant (i) reasonably believe the use of defensive force (ii) to be necessary in the face of an (iii) imminent attack or threat?

The attack, therefore, cannot be a theoretical or hypothetical one, nor can it be a threat that may or will happen sometime in the future. It must be an actual, imminent attack or threat. Acting under official authority relates to the exercise of government authority that makes lawful an act that normally may be considered a criminal act.

An often-cited case of a circumstance involving a "least worst" option is an older English case, *Regina v. Dudley*, involving four people at sea, where one of the four people was purposely killed for the others' survival after they went many days without food or water. After being picked up by a German boat after the killing, some of the individuals on the boat were tried for murder. The defendants argued that the act constituted a justifiable necessity. The English court, however, disagreed. In modern times, American courts have a potential basis to rule that a similar situation may be a justifiable necessity relating to a choice of least worst options. For example, the MPC provides that, "the harm or evil sought to be avoided is greater than that sought to be prevented by the law defining the offense charged." The MPC thus applies a type of cost-benefit analysis when it comes to justifiable necessity.

Insanity Defense

The insanity defense is a criminal law defense that has received a lot of attention and controversy. The insanity defense distinguishes between those individuals who are responsible for their acts and those individuals who are not.

An insanity defense precedent case is the M'Naghten case, a British case in 1843. The case led to the M'Naghten Rule, which held that

> [T]o establish defense on the ground of insanity, it must clearly be proved that, at the time of committing the act, the party accused was laboring under such a defect of reason, from disease of the mind, as not to know the nature and quality of the act he was doing, or if he did know it, that he did not know [that what] he was doing [was] . . . wrong.

The rule is widely adopted by many American courts. In plain English, the M'Naghten Rule focuses on the defendant's cognitive capacity to know and understand his own actions resulting from a mental disease or defect. As a result, the criminal defendant must be unable to comprehend the wrongful nature of the act.

What does the MPC say about the controversial insanity defense? The MPC defines it as a "mental disease or defect" to exclude "an abnormality manifested only by repeated criminal or otherwise antisocial conduct."

Intoxication and Duress

Other criminal law defenses include the defenses of intoxication and duress. To plead an intoxication defense, a person must be too intoxicated to understand his actions. The rationale is that if an individual is intoxicated, then he (defendant) may not be conscious or aware of the risk being created (by the defendant). For the duress defense, a person (defendant) must have committed a crime only because the person (defendant) reasonably believed that doing so was the only way to avoid imminent death or serious bodily injury.

Inchoate Crimes

Can a person be prosecuted even though the crime ended up being incomplete or not at the level of what was originally intended? The short answer is yes. These instances involve inchoate crimes, because the criminal acts were incomplete or imperfect.

The following three types of inchoate crimes exist:

1. **Attempt**: An attempt occurs when a person attempts a criminal act or when she tries to accomplish such an act. The mental element of the crime is the intent to commit the crime. The MPC defines attempt as "a substantial step in a course of conduct," in which the substantial step is "strongly corroborative of the actor's criminal purpose." An example would be buying a gun or knife to commit a criminal act. If the crime is completed, thus no longer being inchoate, then the attempt merges with the related substantive criminal offense.
2. **Solicitation**: A solicitation occurs when the defendant tries to get another person to commit a crime. If the crime is completed, thus no longer being inchoate, then the solicitation merges with the related substantive criminal offense.
3. **Conspiracy**: A conspiracy is an agreement among two or more people with the purpose of committing an unlawful act. In many jurisdictions, and unlike attempt and solicitation, conspiracy does not merge into the inchoate

completed crimes. Thus, it adds an extra layer of punishment to a crime, and it is one of the more commonly used of the three inchoate crimes.

Homicide

One objective of American criminal law is to distinguish between more and less serious criminal offenses, as well as among different levels of severity. Homicide—a broad umbrella term involving the killing of one or more persons—is one criminal law area in which an important objective is to distinguish between different levels of severity among serious crimes.

Homicide can be broadly divided into two subcategories:

1. Murder (divided into first-degree and second-degree murder)
2. Manslaughter (divided into voluntary and involuntary manslaughter)

The traditional definition of murder is the killing of a human being with malice aforethought. Murder is then again divided into first-degree murder and second-degree murder. Distinguishing between first- and second-degree murder is often difficult. The MPC attempts to provide some clarity by essentially eliminating the traditional distinction between the two. Specifically, the MPC defines murder as a killing caused purposely, knowingly, or recklessly "under circumstances manifesting extreme indifference to the value of human life." The MPC then states that "aggravating and mitigating factors" can be considered to determine whether the death penalty should be imposed. Among these factors are considerations not just related to the crime itself, but the person or persons who committed the crime. The defendant's age, past criminal record, and capacity to appreciate or not appreciate the wrongfulness of his acts are among many factors that can be considered.

The second type of homicide—manslaughter—can be thought of as a catch-all crime for nonmurder homicides involving killing a human being without malice aforethought (i.e., manslaughter includes all other types of homicide apart from murder). Manslaughter is then divided again into voluntary and involuntary manslaughter. One major type of voluntary manslaughter involves the killing of another person without malice aforethought under the "heat of passion" caused by a sufficient provocation. An example of this could be when a husband comes home and finds his wife in bed with another man. Finally, involuntary manslaughter exists in which the criminal mental state exists somewhere between extreme recklessness and negligence.

Criminal Procedure

Criminal procedure is the criminal process related to the substantive criminal law issues covered in the previous section. Specifically, it is the process by which crimes are investigated and adjudicated, and where punishment for criminal acts is rendered.

Criminal procedure legal sources can include, among others, the following:

- U.S. Constitution (as well as state constitutions)
- Federal and state case law
- Federal Rules of Criminal Procedure (FRCP) (as well as related state-level rules)

Search and Seizure by the Police

The law of search and seizure governs some basic police investigative techniques. Examples of police search and seizures can occur through actions such as stopping suspected criminals to ask them questions, frisking of a person's clothing and other items, as well as the search of a person's car or home. State search and seizures can also occur through wiretapping, electronic surveillance, examination of garbage (and other items thrown away), as well as through the accessing and auditing of business and/or personal records.

The Fourth Amendment to the U.S. Constitution generally applies to search and seizures conducted by the state, which includes not just police officers, but any government officials who would involve state action. Specifically, the Fourth Amendment prohibits "unreasonable" searches and sets forth the requirements for a court to issue a search warrant, which, among other things, requires that probable cause for the search must exist. A search warrant is evidence of legal authorization from a judge or comparable authority for the police (or other state actor) to conduct a search and, if needed, to seize evidence of a crime.

The U.S. Supreme Court originally held that only physical intrusions constituted a search under the constitutional protections of the Fourth Amendment. Later, the Supreme Court broadened the types of searches to go beyond mere physical intrusions, in a 1976 landmark case, *Katz v. U.S.*, related to a person's reasonable expectation of privacy.

Can all searches be conducted without a search warrant? The short answer is no. Searches must generally be conducted with a search warrant, if the search is deemed to be reasonable. One key indicator of reasonableness is probable cause to believe that evidence of the crime will be found.

Exceptions exist whereby searches can be conducted without a search warrant. One exception relates to seizures of items that are in plain view of the premises in which the search is being conducted. This is known as the plain view doctrine, by which property can be seized without a search warrant or probable cause if it is in plain view (viewable to the eye) during the course of a lawful search by the police or other state actors.

Another exception in which the police or other state actors would not always need a warrant or probable cause relates to a stop and frisk scenario. A stop and frisk typically occurs when an officer briefly stops (detains) a person, often involving questions related to the person's possible knowledge of certain suspicious criminal activity. The police officer would then begin a frisk (patdown) of the person's clothing to make sure that no weapons are in possession by the person who may potentially pose an immediate danger or threat to the police officer.

Throughout the process of search and seizure rights and protection, American courts aim to strike a balance between Fourth Amendment protection of the suspect weighed against allowing the police to perform their duties to protect the public. What if, however, the police conduct an unreasonable search (for instance, without probable cause)? One outcome could be that a court would apply the exclusionary rule, created by a seminal case in 1914, *Weeks v. U.S.* The exclusionary rule states that evidence obtained by the government in violation of the Constitution may not be used against the defendant, because the defendant's constitutional rights have been violated. Thus, any incriminating evidence found during an unreasonable search and seizure, or obtained from a confession, by the state may be excluded from being used as evidence in the prosecution's case. The exclusionary rule is a disincentive for police against conducting unconstitutional searches and seizures, as well as using illegal confession-gathering techniques.

The exclusionary rule has been further extended under the fruit of the poisonous tree doctrine, created by a seminal case in 1920, *Silverthorne Lumber Co. v. U.S.* The fruit of the poisonous tree doctrine extends the exclusionary rule by barring evidence obtained after an illegal search was conducted. However, certain exceptions to the fruit of the poisonous tree doctrine exist, whereby certain illegal evidence can be used, such as evidence obtained in the following conditions:

- Under the good faith exception, whereby an illegal search in which the police reasonably believe in good faith that their search is constitutionally permissible
- The information was discovered by a source independent of the illegal search
- The discovery of information in the illegal search was inevitable
- If the link between the illegal search and evidence discovery is attenuated

Privilege Against Self-Incrimination

In the American criminal system, the prosecution generally has the burden of proving its case through its own efforts, not through the inquisition of the accused (defendant). The U.S. Constitution directly reflects this principle under the Fifth Amendment, which states, "No person . . . shall be compelled in any criminal case to be a witness against himself."

One of the most famous American law cases, *Miranda v. Arizona*, relates to the issue of self-incrimination protections. In the case, the court concluded that it is necessary to use "adequate protective devices . . . to dispel the compulsion inherent in custodial surroundings." In plain English, the court's ruling holds that a person being interrogated by the police should receive adequate protection against the possibility of self-incrimination (to avoid, for instance, an involuntary confession obtained by undue physical force or duress).

This case ultimately led to the formative requirements known as the suspect's Miranda rights against self-incrimination, which requires that the following be stated to the suspect when he or she is detained in custody by the police:

> "[T]hat he has the right to remain silent . . . that anything he says can and will be used against the individual in court . . . that he has the right to consult with a lawyer and to have the lawyer with him during interrogation . . . [and] that if he is indigent, a lawyer will be appointed to represent him."
>
> That if the suspect, "indicates in any manner, at any time prior to or during the questioning, that he wishes to remain silent, the interrogation must cease . . . [and if he] states that he wants an attorney, the interrogation must cease until an attorney is present."

Summary

The field of American criminal law is a complex and controversial subject in both theory and practice. Issues, such as whether the defendant had the requisite mental state (mens rea), along with evidence of the physical act (actus reas) itself, are considered. Alongside these issues are considerations of whether criminal law defenses exist, such as justification and excuses. The killing of another human being is generally categorized as a homicide. Homicides are then divided into the categories of murder (whereby malice aforethought is a necessary element) and manslaughter (whereby malice aforethought is not a necessary element). A defendant may also be prosecuted even if the intended crime was rendered incomplete, under what is known as an inchoate crime.

The field of criminal procedure is the criminal process related to substantive criminal law issues. Specifically, criminal procedure is the process by which crimes are investigated and adjudicated, and where punishment for criminal acts are rendered. Within the area of criminal procedure are issues related to the legality or illegality of search and seizures by the police or other state actors. Most searches must be reasonable and supported by probable cause as evidenced by a search warrant. However, exceptions exist when evidence or confessions obtained illegally can be allowed as evidence in a court of law. The Fourth Amendment, prohibiting illegal search and seizure by the government, aspires to strike a strategic balance between protecting individual freedoms weighed against allowing the police or other state actors to do their job of protecting the people.

INTERNATIONAL BUSINESS LAW: AN AMERICAN LAW PERSPECTIVE

International business law is the division of international law that deals primarily with the rights and regulations of multinational enterprises (MNEs), individuals, and non-governmental organizations (NGOs) as it relates to their cross-border dealings. International business law (IBL) and international public law (IPL) share substantial common ground. For example, much like with IPL, IBL rests on the common foundation of general international law principles.

IBL and IPL can be distinguished in terms of actor types and the types of activities in which actors engage. IBL focuses more attention on the rights and responsibilities of MNEs, states, individuals, and NGOs. Some examples of IBL include contracts, money and banking, finance, securities regulation, intellectual property, antitrust, and taxation.

When International Law Is Binding

The issue of when international law is binding is the same whether for IBL or IPL. Specifically, the general rule is that international law is binding only upon those parties that consent to the jurisdiction of international law. Jurisdiction is defined as the court's legal authority to hear a particular legal dispute between two or more parties.

In addition to the consent issue with the International Court of Justice (ICJ), consent is also, but not always, required for jurisdiction relating to other tribunals. The use of arbitration panels is especially relevant for IBL, in which MNEs, NGOs, and individuals may have standing to bring forth a suit. In addition to the ICJ, municipal domestic courts also have the option to apply IBL. Specifically relating to IBL cases, some domestic courts, most notably U.S. courts, can establish jurisdiction over parties that do not expressly consent to its jurisdiction.

International Business Law: Entity Types

As previously mentioned, IBL is composed of several smaller categories, including MNEs, foreign investment, securities regulation, money and banking, and trade. Each of these categories could be discussed at an intricate level, but for purposes of this chapter, a broad overview of each category is given, from the perspective of entity types.

Multinational Enterprises

A multinational enterprise (MNE) is defined as an entity that conducts business in two or more states. The irony of an MNE is that this entity begins at the domestic level under municipal domestic law, not under international law. Moreover, in theory, an entity's principal place of business (PPB; i.e., the physical building(s) and employees of the entity) and state of registration (filing of an entity's articles of incorporation to a particular state-level agency) may be in the same state (e.g., Delaware). In practice, however, an entity's PPB and state of registration can be in separate states. The most common example is in the U.S. case, whereby many MNEs are registered in the state of Delaware, with a PPB in the state of New York or New Jersey.

Regarding MNEs, the type of business structure that various organizations are registered as represents a critical IBL issue. In total, three types of business structures exist, as follows:

1. Sole proprietorships
2. Partnerships
3. Stock corporations

Each of these three types is discussed in following sections. As background, when focusing on the three various business structure types, four critical issues exist to distinguish one business type from another. The first critical issue is the level of liability; that is, whether the person(s) involved in the business structure have limited or unlimited liability. The second critical issue is how much each investor/owner receives for her or his financial contributions to this business type. The third critical issue is whether the owner/investor(s) involved are distinguishable or indistinguishable from the business entity itself. The fourth and final critical issue is the tax treatment type that the business entity is subject to and/or entitled to receive.

Sole Proprietorships

Sole proprietorships exist when a single person forms an entity to conduct a business (i.e., as a service or goods provider). In a sole proprietorship, depending on the jurisdiction, the sole proprietor may or may not need to file registration documents with a particular state agency.

In terms of liability, the sole proprietor generally has unlimited liability relating to any gains/losses of the sole proprietorship. This means that if a sole proprietor invests $100, then the sole proprietor is subject to any amount of liability (i.e., below, at, or exceeding $100). The upside exists in that a sole proprietor receives any and all financial returns from the sole proprietorship (i.e., below, at, or above the sole proprietor's original $100 financial contribution). Moreover, the sole proprietor is viewed as indistinguishable from the sole proprietorship. In other words, the sole owner/investor can generally be viewed as one and the same as his or her sole proprietorship, which links into the next and final critical issue.

In terms of tax treatment, the sole proprietorship and the sole proprietor generally do not pay separate taxes. Instead, the two are merged so that the sole proprietor pays and files only one tax return. This means that any gains/losses from the sole proprietorship are simply placed onto that sole proprietor's individual tax returns. The rationale is that this approach is a simpler and easier method by which to file taxes from the perspectives of both the sole proprietor and the sole proprietorship.

Partnerships

Partnerships exist when two or more individuals decide to form a business together that is not incorporated.

In general, the following two types of partnerships exist:

1. Limited partnerships
2. Unlimited (general) partnerships

In a limited partnership, the partnership is typically composed of at least one or more individual(s) who maintain limited liability (i.e., where liability is capped at the amount of the partner's monetary contribution) and at least one or more person(s) who maintain unlimited liability (i.e., where liability is not capped, and thus, can potentially exceed the partner's monetary contribution).

In terms of determining partnership payments, a legal document known as a partnership agreement governs the partnership. The partnership agreement is effectively a legal contract, and much like a contract, the partnership agreement sets forth the terms and conditions of how the partnership will operate at a practical level. For example, a typical partnership agreement may set forth such things as the partnership's mission statement, the induction and exit process of partners, the amount of required monetary contribution by each partner, the dissolution of the partnership, and processes for amending the partnership agreement.

Typically, however, an unlimited liability (general) partner who is exposed to potentially unlimited legal and economic risk is rewarded vis-à-vis a higher potential monetary benefit, as set forth in the partnership agreement. Similarly, a limited liability partner who is exposed to relatively less legal and economic risk will therefore most likely be entitled to a smaller potential monetary benefit, as set forth in the partnership agreement. In other words, much like the principles underlying the free market system, a partner will invest in a particular partnership based on the view that the potential benefits outweigh the potential costs of that particular association.

Moreover, the partners in this business type are generally not viewed as strictly separate from the partnership, much like in the case with sole proprietors who are not viewed as distinct from their sole proprietorships. From a tax perspective, however, the partnership is taxed as an entity separate and distinct from the partners, although partners should include in their personal taxes (separate from the partnership's tax) any and all income gained from the partnership.

Public Stock Corporations

A public stock corporation is a business entity type that is incorporated, can raise money through the international financial markets, and whose owners are separate and distinct from the corporate entity itself.

To form a public stock corporation, an entity must file a legal document known as the entity's articles of incorporation with a specific state business registration agency in what is referred to as incorporation. The purpose of articles of incorporation is to effectively create and define the public stock corporation. The rationale behind this procedure is to provide the state with relevant information related to the business entity in the event that an inquiry must be made. Another rationale is that because a public stock corporation can acquire funding through the marketplace, these entities can potentially render greater harm to the public. Therefore, the state focuses relatively greater scrutiny toward public stock corporations in comparison to partnerships and sole proprietorships.

Public stock corporations also benefit from having the option to acquire funding through financial (capital) markets. In this way, public stock corporations are distinguishable from partnerships and sole proprietorships, in which both are unable to procure direct external funding. A typical example of acquiring funding is when an issuer (i.e., the business entity that is issuing a financial instrument) issues shares (i.e., equity ownership of the issuer) to global investors in exchange for a predetermined amount of money.

A share, also referred to as stock or equity, essentially represents a designated percentage ownership interest of the issuer. In form, a share is merely a piece of paper that states relevant information about the issuer and the product (share) itself. In substance, a share is a type of legal agreement between the issuer and the legal owner of the share (shareholder). For example, hypothetically speaking, if Samsung

Electronics issues 100 shares, and Investor A buys 10 shares (and assuming that Samsung Electronics has 100 total outstanding shares upon issue date), then Investor A effectively owns 10 percent of Samsung Electronics (i.e., 10 shares out of a possible 100 total outstanding shares).

In a public stock corporation structure, the legal owners (shareholders) are viewed as separate and distinct from the corporate entity itself, whereby a corporate entity is referred to as a juridical entity, from the court's view. For this reason, the shareholders have limited liability, and furthermore, the shareholders have a legal right to bring suit against the corporate (juridical) entity itself, referred to as a shareholder's derivative suit, in the event of egregious and/or willful misconduct on behalf of a corporate entity. For example, if Investor A (shareholder) owns 10 percent of Company A's shares, valued at $1 million, then Investor A's maximum loss amount is generally capped at no more than $1 million.

The main benefits of a public stock corporation are greater funding opportunities vis-à-vis financial markets and limited liability of owners/shareholders. The main downsides of a public stock corporation are increased state and/or regulatory scrutiny, the requirement of disclosing the corporation's financial statements to the public, and potential shareholder derivative suits (i.e., a lawsuit in which a corporate shareholder sues the directors, management, or other shareholders of the issuer corporate entity).

Examples of MNEs and IBL in practice exist in several landmark cases. In *Puerto Rico v. Russell*, the U.S. Supreme Court considered the issue of whether a sociedad en commandita (from Spanish, meaning "limited partnership") under civil law had standing to bring suit in U.S. courts under common law. The second issue considered was whether Russell, an entity created under the laws of Puerto Rico, not the United States, constituted a juridical entity, whereby the entity's owners are distinct from the company itself. The court's conclusion was a no ruling to both issues. Thus, the U.S. Supreme Court refused to hear the case and remanded the case to the Puerto Rican Insular Court (i.e., back to the Puerto Rican municipal courts).

A separate case, known as *Barcelona, Traction, Light, and Power Company, Ltd, (Belgium v. Spain)* I.C.J. 1970 I.C.J. 3, represents another seminal IBL case. In the Barcelona case, the ICJ considered whether Belgium had standing (i.e., a legal right to bring forth a suit) against Spain for losses suffered by Belgium shareholders, whereby the Belgium shareholders owned a combined total of 88 percent of Barcelona Traction's total outstanding shares. Much like in the Russell case, the ICJ in the Barcelona case considered the issue of whether the entity, Barcelona Traction, constituted a juridical entity. If the ICJ had held yes to this issue, then Belgium would have had standing to bring suit in the ICJ. The rationale is that with a juridical entity, only the state in which the entity is registered and incorporated has standing to bring suit. In the case, Barcelona Traction was incorporated in Canada, not Belgium. Therefore, only Canada had standing to bring forth suit in the ICJ. Thus, the case was dismissed.

Foreign Investment

Foreign investment is a strategy used by various countries to help with capital flows into local economies. Put simply, foreign investment occurs when foreign entities (i.e., states, MNEs, and/or individuals) invest in another country's markets. The rationale for this is that the additional capital into a local economy will help with domestic job creation and technology transfer. The downside is the argument that foreign capital may lead to undue influence on the local economy, displace local jobs, and disrupt local industries.

As a result of arguments relating to foreign investment, both pros and cons, different policy initiatives exist. These policies are typically set by a state's government, because governments represent the state's predominant gatekeeper that can allow or not allow foreign capital into its borders. Two main strategies exist to bring foreign capital into a domestic economy. The first strategy is the implementation of free zones, which include such things as free trade areas, free trade zones, subzones, and export processing zones. The second strategy is the implementation of various guarantees, which include such things as foreign investment guarantees, repatriation guarantees, and nondiscrimination guarantees.

Free Zones

A free zone is a government-designated geographic area that is free from customs, import taxes, and tariffs. In this area, goods can be imported and exported free of import and export restrictions that would normally be placed in nonfree zones.

A free trade area (FTA) is a designated geographic area agreed upon by two or more states. Within FTAs, customs and tariffs are either reduced or eliminated relating to predetermined goods and services between the two states. In other words, an FTA functions in much the same way as a free zone, except that an FTA occurs between two states at the international level, whereas a free zone exchange of goods and/or services can occur at the national or international level. A free trade zone (FTZ) is simply a free zone located in or near a port city. A subzone is a free zone type that closely resembles an FTZ but is geographically distinct from it.

An export processing zone (EPZ) is a subzone type in which foreign goods are manufactured near border cities for export to another country free of customs, tariffs, and duties. EPZs are popular particularly with developing economies to attract foreign MNEs into their markets. A classic EPZ example exists in the maquiladora programs along the Mexico–U.S. border, in which many U.S. firms have set up manufacturing bases on the Mexican side of the border for cheap labor and custom-free export of goods into the U.S. market. The United States gains because MNEs can manufacture their products relatively cheaper, leveraging cheaper labor costs and lower or no imposed customs. Mexico also gains because the creation of U.S. manufacturing centers in Mexico provides much-needed jobs for the Mexican economy.

Nissan Motor Mfg. Corp. USA v. United States represents a famous case relating to free zones. In the case, a U.S. federal court held that Nissan (plaintiff) must pay customs duties to the United States for the import of certain high-tech automobile manufacturing machinery into a subzone. The court's rationale was that the import of machinery did not fall under the many custom exemptions listed in the Free Trade Zones Act of 1934 and its subsequent 1950 amendment. As a result, Nissan had to pay approximately $3 million in assessed duties.

Guarantees

Two main types of guarantees exist to help bring foreign investment into a particular local economy. The first type is called a repatriation guarantee, which ensures that any foreign investor (individual, MNE, or government) can repatriate any capital and profit earned from an investment. The second type is called a nondiscrimination guarantee, which ensures that foreign investors will be treated in the same way as the host state's local investors. A host nation government may provide guarantees either separately or together based on its sole discretion.

Securities Regulation

Securities regulation is defined as the body of laws and rules that oversee securities. Securities are traded in what is called the securities market. A security is broadly defined as a share, participation, bond, or any other interest in an entity or other property. A stock (equity), as mentioned, represents a certain percentage ownership interest of a particular issuing company. As a result, certain rights and obligations exist in relating to owning a stock, such as the right to vote in shareholder meetings and distribution of assets upon dissolution of the issuing company. A bond is effectively a contractual obligation by the issuer to repay the bondholder the principal amount (at the bond's maturity date) and interest payments (at specified interest payment periods during the bond's life).

An alternative way to think of a bond is as a loan given to the issuer by the bondholder. The bondholder has an economic incentive in the form of interest payments to make a loan. Here, the bond issuer has an incentive to pay the interest amount, because the issuer takes the view that paying extra interest later to receive the loan principal amount now is worthwhile. Thus, both parties can potentially benefit, which is the ideal situation in any securities transaction.

A securities exchange is the marketplace forum where securities are bought and sold. When a party enters into transactions in a securities exchange, the party is typically either a buyer or a seller. The securities exchange effectively acts as the meeting place at which buyers and sellers can get together and trade. Within any given trade, the buyer takes the view that he or she can resell the security at a higher price than his or her purchase price in the short or long run. Conversely, the seller is effectively either profit-taking by selling the security (i.e., by selling at a price higher than the security's purchase price) or minimizing losses (i.e., has lost money on the security's sale, but is selling now because he or she is taking the view that losses may be greater later than now by not selling now).

In terms of case law relating to securities regulation, two classic cases exist. In *Batchelder v. Kawamoto*, a U.S. federal court ruled on a dispute relating to the holder of American depository receipts (ADRs), which reflects ownership of shares, relating to a foreign entity, Honda Japan. The interesting aspect of the Kawamoto case is that, in its legal analysis, the U.S. court referred to and applied Japanese business law in the case, in addition to U.S. (New York) law. Specifically, the court analyzed Article 267 of the Japanese Commercial Code that regulated shareholder rights to see if an ADR holder was a shareholder under that provision. This case demonstrates that U.S. courts can apply non-U.S. foreign law in addition to U.S. law with regards to at least securities regulation, reflecting the international flavor of financial transactions today. This case also typifies how business, including international finance, and legal issues can intersect in the international arena in both theory and practice.

The second notable case relating to securities regulation is *United States v. O'Hagan*. In the O'Hagan case, the court expanded the definition of "insider" relating to a U.S. federal insider trading law, under 10(b) and (10)(b)(5) of the Securities and Exchange Act of 1934. The case involved O'Hagan (defendant), who was a lawyer working for a law firm that represented an American firm (Pillsbury), although O'Hagan was not the lawyer working on behalf of Pillsbury. In the case, Grand Met (a non-U.S. firm) was in negotiations for the takeover of Pillsbury. These negotiations constituted confidential nonpublic information that should not have been used for personal gain under the above laws, but O'Hagan, contrary to these laws, used this confidential nonpublic information to purchase substantial amounts of Pillsbury shares and other interests. Thereafter, O'Hagan sold the Pillsbury shares for a $4.3 million profit. The U.S. Supreme Court ruled for the United States (plaintiff) and against O'Hagan (defendant), and in the process, notably expanded the definition of "insider" to include, among others, lawyers, accountants, and consultants (above and beyond typical corporate directors and similar parties).

Money and Banking

A landmark American law case relating to money and banking exists with the U.S. Supreme Court's ruling in *Republic of Argentina v. Weltover*. This case focuses on two overlapping issues of money and banking, as well as choice of law tribunals. In this case, the U.S. Supreme Court considered the issue of whether it had jurisdiction over a dispute in which all parties (both plaintiff and defendant) were non-U.S. residents.

The dispute related to the Republic of Argentina's bond issuance (Defendant Issuer) to several global bondholders (Plaintiff Investors) and Defendant Issuer's subsequent failure to pay debts owed under bond instruments to the Plaintiff Investors. The court held that even if all litigants were non-U.S. residents, U.S. federal courts could still exercise jurisdiction in the case to subsequently hear the dispute on its merits.

Another aspect of money and banking is the international financial system. The international financial system can be separated into two distinct time periods: pre- and post–gold bullion standard system periods.

The pre–gold bullion standard period officially ended in 1976, when the International Monetary Fund (IMF), an international organization created in 1944, passed its

IMF Second Amendment system, which allowed states to value their currency in terms of nongold references. Up to that point, many states relied on the gold standard system, where a state's national currency's value was fixed to a predetermined amount of gold bullion. The main benefit of the gold bullion standard was supposed international monetary stability, because printed currency had to be supported by a certain amount of gold reserves. Thus, the greater a state's gold reserves, the more national currency a state could print. Conversely, a state that had relatively fewer gold reserves would be more restricted in terms of how much national currency it could print.

The gold bullion standard worked fine in both theory and practice up until World War I (1914–1919) and the Great Depression (1930s). One rationale for the gold standard's success, apart from those two main time periods, is that the system was never stress-tested. In all other time periods, apart from World War I and the Great Depression in the early 20th century, there existed relative economic stability. The advent of World War I and the Great Depression, however, brought out a glaring weakness in the gold bullion system. The system was too rigid and inflexible in times of financial uncertainty because of the following issues:

- Printed money was constrained by the amount of gold held.
- Governments tend to increase national spending and, therefore, print more money in times of financial uncertainty.
- The world's gold supply was fixed, but a nation's printed money supply was not fixed, meaning that the rigid system when placed under severe economic pressure would ultimately collapse when trying to print more money to stimulate the economy. Because of the gold bullion system, however, a government's gold supply could not keep pace with its printing of money, and thus, must either decide whether to opt out of the gold bullion system or cease printing more needed money due to the inherent constraints of the gold standard.

Both options seemed unfeasible, so many states such as Great Britain pulled out of the gold bullion system during severe economic cycle periods. In effect, the IMF Second Amendment in 1976 put into writing what many states already clearly understood: The gold bullion system simply did not work. Furthermore, a more flexible system was needed in which a state's national currency could be valued in nongold terms. This event, therefore, marked a defining moment within the world's international financial infrastructure, which affected world markets, including the global trade regime.

The World Trade Organization (WTO) and International Trade

International trade law (ITL) is a subdivision of IBL and can be defined as the body of rules and regulations relating to the fostering and regulation of exchanging goods and services. The main distinguishing characteristic from IBL is that ITL focuses primarily on the World Trade Organization (WTO), an international organization created to help foster international trade. The WTO's foundation also marks the beginning of modern ITL. Thus, to understand modern ITL, an understanding of the WTO and its various functions are beneficial and value-added skill sets.

As background, the WTO's predecessor existed in the form of the General Agreement on Trade and Tariffs (GATT), which was formed shortly after the end of World War II (1945) and governed under the auspices of a legal instrument called GATT 1947. GATT was replaced after the GATT Uruguay Round (related to trade negotiations held in Uruguay) in 1994 by the WTO. The WTO is governed under the auspices of a legal instrument known as the WTO Agreement.

The WTO has four distinct purposes:

1. Implement and carry out the WTO Agreement.
2. Act as a multilateral forum for international trade negotiations.
3. Serve as a dispute resolution tribunal.
4. Review the trade policies and practices of the WTO and its members.

One European case that focuses on international trade law and GATT 1947's application to domestic law relates to *Finance Ministry v. Manifattura*. In the case, the Italian Court of Cassation considered the issue of whether GATT 1947 was directly effective on Italian domestic law. If an international agreement, including GATT 1947, is considered to be directly effective, then no domestic legislation is generally needed to make the provisions of an international agreement part of that signatory state's domestic municipal law. Conversely, if an international agreement, including GATT 1947, is considered not to be directly effective, then domestic legislation is generally needed to make provisions of an international agreement part of that signatory state's domestic law. The Italian court, applying international trade law, concluded that GATT 1947 was directly effective, and therefore was not a simple declaration of principle.

Summary

International business law (IBL) from an American law perspective is defined as the division of international law that deals primarily with the rights and regulations of multinational enterprises, states, individuals, and nongovernmental organizations as it relates to their cross-border dealings. Examples of IBL include foreign investment, securities regulation, money and banking, and trade. Because IBL actors are having a more profound influence on global affairs, the overlapping features of IBL provide a unique and value-added skill set, which can be effectively leveraged from both an academic and professional perspective. This unique knowledge skill set includes the keen knowledge of IBL issues, such as entity business types, securities regulations, cross-border financial transactions, and international trade agreements, which, viewed separately and collectively, can positively impact many organizations and events around the world.

INTERNATIONAL PUBLIC LAW: AN AMERICAN LAW PERSPECTIVE

The previous chapter discussed international business law, but what is international public law (IPL)? The traditional definition of IPL typically covered only states, which are broadly defined as having a defined territory, fixed population, and a government. In contrast, the post-1945 modern definition of IPL covers not only states, but also includes multinational corporations (MNCs), individuals, intergovernmental organizations (IGOs), and nongovernmental organizations (NGOs). The big picture is that modern international law covers many more actors than traditional international law. The rationale is that, in the post-1945 era, actors like MNCs, individuals, IGOs, and NGOs possessed relatively more potential to both benefit as well as harm the global arena.

The Modern View of International Public Law

The year 1945, and the end of World War II, marked the beginning of modern international law. Before 1945, international law was traditionally viewed as applying only to states.

A state is defined as an entity that has the following:

- A fixed population
- A defined territory
- A government that is capable of (a) governing its fixed population and defined territory and (b) entering into international relations

Following 1945, however, the purview of international public law expanded greatly into a modern definition of international law—specifically, to include states, as well as international organizations (including both IGOs and NGOs), individuals, and MNEs. Arguably, one of the most prominent international public law institutions today is the United Nations, which is described in the next section.

The United Nations

One of the most defining institutions created following World War II was the United Nations (UN). The creation of the UN was in response to the many acts perpetrated during World War II that shocked the conscience of the international community.

The UN has the following four main purposes:

1. Maintain peace throughout the world.
2. Develop friendly relations among nations.
3. Help nations work together to improve the lives of poor people, to conquer hunger, disease, and illiteracy, and to encourage respect for each other's rights and freedoms.
4. Be a center for harmonizing the actions of nations to achieve these goals.

The UN's constituent instrument is known as the UN Charter. The UN Charter sets forth, among other things, the UN's scope and duty, procedural issues, and membership qualifications. The UN Charter in effect encapsulates much of the body and spirit of international public law. As of 2014, the UN Charter has 193 signatory states, representing nearly every major region of the world. Because of the high number of state signatory parties, and the diverse composition of these state parties, the UN Charter signatory state number of 193 is viewed as a benchmark by which other international conventions and agreements are compared.

Much like a large parent company, the UN also has several subsidiary-type bodies, known as UN organs. These UN organs include the Secretariat (the primary public relations organ, which reviews reports and makes recommendations), the General Assembly (the primary legislative body), the Security Council (which has the authority to use force to preserve peace and security), and the International Court of Justice (ICJ; the main judicial organ).

When Is International Law Binding?

A common question that international law students pose is: When is international law binding? The general rule is that international law is binding on those parties that consent to the jurisdiction of international law. For example, relating to the ICJ, generally only those member states that consent to the ICJ's jurisdiction are bound by the rights and privileges of ICJ judicial decisions, although as with many aspects of law, exceptions exist.

Because the ICJ is the main judicial organ of the UN, does this mean that all UN member states are deemed to have automatically consented to ICJ jurisdiction? The short answer is no. Consent to being a UN member state and consenting to ICJ jurisdiction are two separate but related issues. Put differently, ICJ member states are a subset of the total population of UN member states. Another question may be: Why would states consent to ICJ jurisdiction? One reason is that states, acting rationally in the furtherance of their own self-interest, would consent to ICJ jurisdiction based on the working assumption that they believe that the benefits outweigh the costs of consenting to ICJ jurisdiction.

Benefits often include the ability to bring forth a cause of action (i.e., a lawsuit) as plaintiff against another state. In some cases, this benefit would help smaller and/or weaker states. The costs, however, often include being a defendant. Since the inception of both the UN and ICJ following World War II, the United States has been a UN member state and originally consented to ICJ jurisdiction. However, in 1984, related to a seminal case, *Nicaragua v. United States*, the United States lost a case to Nicaragua and subsequently chose to give notice of its withdrawal from ICJ jurisdiction. In other words, as part of its calculations, the United States may have perceived that the benefits no longer outweighed the costs of ICJ jurisdiction.

The practical effect of this decision, and the subsequent withdrawal by the United States from the ICJ, is that the United States generally is no longer able to use the ICJ as a forum to sue and be sued. Another concern is the signal that is being sent by the United States when withdrawing from the ICJ. Specifically, it may become more difficult to compel other nations to reconstitute their legal systems to international norms when the United States is not a party to arguably the most notable international public law tribunal. From the ICJ perspective, the withdrawal of U.S. consent to ICJ jurisdiction diminishes the ICJ's credibility within the international community, because many members of the international community view U.S. participation as a critical credibility benchmark.

The primary tribunal discussed thus far relating to the consent issue is the ICJ. However, apart from the ICJ, consent is also required for jurisdiction relating to other tribunals, such as arbitration panels. Moreover, municipal courts, including U.S. courts, can establish jurisdiction in certain cases over parties that do not expressly consent to its jurisdiction. One classic example of this scenario exists with a case, *Filartiga v. Pena-Irala*, whereby a U.S. court concluded it had jurisdiction to hear a dispute relating to gross human rights violations in which all litigants were non-U.S. parties, whereby the defendant did not expressly consent to jurisdiction.

International Law Tribunal Types

Several international law tribunal types exist. The main types are as follows:

- International Court of Justice (ICJ)
- International Criminal Court (ICC)

- International arbitration panels
- Municipal courts

International Court of Justice

The International Court of Justice (ICJ) is the main judicial organ of the United Nations. The practical effect is that the ICJ is used as one of the main UN organs to settle legal disputes between UN member states that have consented to ICJ jurisdiction.

The ICJ was formed in 1945, following the end of World War II, and was modeled after the Permanent Court of International Justice, which functioned as the judicial organ of the League of Nations from 1920 to 1939. The League of Nations was the pre-1945 predecessor to the UN. UN member states are generally members of the ICJ; however, ICJ member states may elect to fully consent to the ICJ's jurisdiction or consent with reservations, whereby a state consents to ICJ jurisdiction in principle, but with certain exceptions and/or qualifications. An ICJ member state may also choose to withdraw from ICJ jurisdiction, as in the U.S. case discussed earlier. The main constituent document that prescribe the rules and regulations relating to the scope and internal procedures of the ICJ are set forth in the Statute of the International Court of Justice (ICJ Statute).

As the main judicial organ of the UN, the ICJ hears legal disputes between member states. The ICJ is composed of 15 judges. At first glance, 15 ICJ judges may seem like an overly high number to hear a particular dispute, but this high number helps ensure that the 193 UN signatories are represented to the greatest extent possible.

The ICJ Statute, as earlier mentioned, is the main constituent instrument of the ICJ. In ICJ Statute Article 38(1), the sources of international law are provided, which are as follows:

- International conventions, which often encompasses treaties
- International customs, which often encompasses regional customs
- General principles of law of "civilised nations"
- Scholars and noted authorities ("the most highly qualified publicists")

The ICJ provides two general types of international law remedies:

- Binding, nonadvisory judicial decisions, based on the ICJ's "contentious" jurisdiction
- Nonbinding advisory opinions, based on the ICJ's "advisory" jurisdiction

The ICJ generally only hears disputes between states, in what is known as the ICJ's contentious jurisdiction. This also means that any nonstate actors, such as individuals, IGOs, NGOs, or MNEs, could not directly bring suit in the ICJ. In other words, MNE of State A could not directly sue State B in the ICJ.

This does not, however, automatically mean that there is no possibility for a wronged individual, for example, to have his or her case heard in the ICJ. One legal solution exists through state sponsorship, which takes place when the state sponsors an individual, MNE, or other relevant entity that resides or is domiciled, respectively, in that particular state. The net effect of state sponsorship is that the alleged injury to the individual or MNE of State A becomes an injury of State A as a result of the individual's residency or entity's domicile or presence in State A. Cases of state sponsorship are, however, more the exception than the general rule, because more state sponsorship requests exist than can be given by any particular state.

International Criminal Court

The International Criminal Court (ICC) is an independent international organization to the UN. The ICC was established by the Rome Statute of the International Criminal Court (Rome Statute). The ICC represents the first-ever permanent, treaty-based, international criminal court created to ensure the rule of law relating to egregious international crimes that "shock the conscience" of the international community.

The ICC is distinguishable from the ICJ in three main respects. First, the ICC can hear cases related to nonstates. The most notable example exists in that the ICC can hear complaints related to the criminal acts of individuals, such as the alleged acts of genocide and war crimes against Slobodan Milosevic. In other words, nonstate actors can be haled into the ICC's jurisdiction. Second, the ICC's focus deals with criminal cases related to genocide and war crimes, whereas the ICJ's purview is much broader. Thus, the ICC can hear disputes relating to broader subject matters. Third, the ICJ is the UN's main judicial organ, whereas the ICC is technically independent of the UN.

Much like the ICJ Statute with respect to the ICJ, the ICC's Rome Statute sets out the ICC's jurisdiction, structure, and functions. Any person who commits any of the crimes listed under the Rome Statute can be held liable for ICC prosecution. As of 2014, 122 countries were state parties to the Rome Statute. Out of the 122 signatory states, 34 are from Africa, 18 are from the Asia-Pacific region, 18 are from Eastern Europe, 27 are from Latin America and the Caribbean, and 25 are from Western Europe and other states.

The ICC can establish jurisdiction relating to crimes of genocide, crimes against humanity, and war crimes, all of which are defined under the Rome Statute. The ICC also has jurisdiction over natural persons aged 18 and older. Moreover, official capacity as a head of state, a member of a government or parliament, an elected representative, or a government official does not exempt a person from criminal responsibility under the ICC. Commanders and superiors relating to military and paramilitary regimes can potentially also be held liable for criminal offenses committed by forces under their effective command and control or effective authority and control under the ICC.

Other Tribunals: International Arbitration Panels and Municipal Courts

Apart from the ICJ and ICC, other international law tribunals exist in both theory and practice in the form of international arbitration panels and municipal courts. International arbitration tribunals allow for litigants to have a dispute heard by an impartial third party, referred to as the arbitrator. The arbitrator's decision is typically binding. The main benefit of arbitration is less time, money, and reputational risk, because the dispute is heard privately among the parties, outside of the public court system. The main downside of arbitration is that the arbitration panel's decision may, in certain circumstances, be appealable. Furthermore, arbitration panels can apply aspects of international law if relevant issues exist, and if the parties consent.

Municipal domestic courts represent another tribunal type that can apply international public law. This concept may seem counterintuitive, because the common perception is that municipal courts apply only the law of their respective jurisdiction. Numerous examples, however, exist in the form of case law, in which municipal courts apply aspects of international law. In fact, one notable U.S. Supreme Court judge famously declared that "international law is our [American] law."

International Public Law's Global Impact

Modern IPL was beneficial in that it helped address the acts of Nazi Germany and Imperial Japan during World War II, which were unanimously viewed as egregious, blatantly counter to the peace and security of the world, and in gross violation of basic human rights. Thus, the international community came together in support of various IPL tribunals to render justice for aggrieved parties, namely the Nuremberg Trials and the Tokyo War Crimes Trials. The creation of tribunals and the subsequent successful prosecution of various involved war criminals sent a clear and resounding message to the world that such acts would no longer be tolerated under modern IPL.

Another prime example of the impact of IPL includes the trial of Slobodan Milosevic. As background, in 1992, Bosnia declared its independence from Yugoslavia. With the support of the Yugoslav army, Bosnian Serbs rebelled against the secession, sparking a war among Bosnian Serbs, Muslims, and Croats that resulted in the deaths of tens of thousands of people. Afterward, the International Criminal Tribunal for the former Yugoslavia charged Slobodan Milosevic, the former Serbian leader, with international human rights crimes for the deaths of about 7,500 Muslims by Bosnian Serbs. Evidence strongly suggested that the acts were part of a master plan of "ethnic cleansing," designed and controlled by Milosevic, to create a pure greater Serbia devoid of non-Serbs.

In the case, the prosecutor argued that Milosevic's acts constituted a gross violation of international human rights law, including (1) acts of genocide and (2) violations of fundamental freedoms of individuals. Milosevic (defendant), acting in his own defense as a pro se litigant, argued that he is not liable for such acts because (1) the alleged acts of genocide of the Bosnian Serbs and its military were beyond his control; and (2) even assuming he was in control of the Bosnian Serbs and its military, such acts were based on nationalism rather than racism or religious discrimination; therefore, according to Milosevic, no violations of fundamental freedoms existed. The Milosevic case is an illustration of how alleged injustices to humankind are not only historic but are also ongoing in the current day. Thus, IPL clearly helps place a strong check and balance on alleged violators of international law before, during, and after the occurrence of egregious acts.

Apart from gross human rights violations and infringements of peace and security are denial of justice issues. One of the more referred-to cases relating to the denial of justice is *Chattin v. United Mexican States*. In *Chattin*, the Mexican court majority applied international standards in concluding that certain acts by Mexico constituted a denial of justice to Mr. Chattin, a U.S. citizen employed in Mexico.

Separate from the denial of justice, IPL also helps address key environmental law issues. Two cases illustrate this point. The first case, *United States v. Canada* (Trail Smelter Arbitration case) involved a dispute before an arbitration panel relating to the release of certain toxins into the air and riverbeds from a Canadian city located just 10 miles north of the Canada–U.S. border to the U.S. border state of Washington. The majority in the Trail Smelter Arbitration case held for the U.S. (plaintiff) and concluded that Canada (defendant) was both liable for monetary damages, and, further, was ordered to refrain from releasing further pollutant emissions. In doing so, the arbitration tribunal held that a duty existed for states to not infringe upon the sovereign rights of other states to a pollutant-free environment, a landmark holding within environmental law at the time (from the 1930s to the early 1940s).

The second seminal case, *Australia v. France* (the Nuclear Tests case), related to the nuclear weapons tests in 1972 and 1973 by France off of a South Pacific French territory near Australia. Australia brought suit in the ICJ against France in 1973. In probable direct response, France discontinued its nuclear tests in 1973, and the ICJ suit was not further pursued. These cases demonstrate that IPL has both theoretical and practical significance that forces parties to act in conformity with IPL involving some of the most serious issues facing humankind.

Summary

International public law is defined as the rules and regulations regarding activities between two or more states. The year 1945 marked the end of World War II and the beginning of modern public international law. Under the modern view in the post-1945 period, international public law covers states, organizations, multinational enterprises, and individuals. The United Nations Charter embodies much of the spirit and substance underlying international public law. Moreover, the International Court of Justice is one of the more visible international public law tribunals, which seeks to resolve disputes between states.

ALTERNATIVE DISPUTE RESOLUTION AND CIVIL LITIGATION

Most cases in the American legal system are resolved out of the courtroom through alternative dispute resolution (ADR) before the dispute is brought into the courtroom through the civil litigation process. This chapter discusses various aspects of ADR and then focuses on the civil litigation process. In this process, ADR options (namely, mediation) can be set aside, temporarily or entirely, for a court-based civil litigation process and ruling.

Alternative Dispute Resolution

Alternative dispute resolution is a broad term attached to various methods of resolving disputes within the American legal system, including, but not limited to, arbitration, mediation, and negotiation. Each of these ADR approaches is covered in this section.

Arbitration

Arbitration represents one type of dispute resolution. It is often used to resolve disputes to get to a yes or no final determination on a particular issue or issues. Typically, arbitration is used when mediation has not been chosen or has failed. Although states can be involved in arbitration proceedings, private parties also are free to enter into arbitration proceedings so long as all relevant parties consent to arbitration proceedings.

Arbitration involves an impartial third party—referred to as the arbitrator—who renders a decision relating to a specific issue or issues in a dispute between two or more parties. The number of arbitrators varies, where having one, two, three, or even more arbitrators would be the norm, although they are usually in odd numbers to avoid an evenly split judgment. Each arbitrator is generally chosen by one or more of the relevant parties to the dispute, often selected based on the arbitrator's knowledge and expertise in a field related to the dispute, which can include current or former attorneys, judges, academics, and/or other relevant experts.

An arbitration proceeding can be distinguished from a legal action heard by judges in a court in that an arbitration proceeding is typically private, whereas litigation in a court is typically public in nature. Thus, one benefit of a private proceeding, as in the case of arbitration, is that outside parties not directly related to the dispute are normally not allowed to listen in on the proceedings. This generally includes members of the press, and possibly other industry members, in which public disclosure (and even the mere public appearance in a lawsuit dispute) can result in less than positive consequences. For example, an article could be printed in a financial news publication that a particular lawsuit proceeding has commenced between two large firms, which could clearly have potentially negative effects on stock prices.

The parties to an arbitration proceeding also generally can decide whether the arbitration decision is binding on the parties as well as whether the opinion is appealable or nonappealable. The parties often opt for a nonappealable arbitration decision, because this can decrease the amount of time involved in the dispute before a final outcome is rendered. In contrast, in a public court system, depending on which court is the court of first instance to hear the dispute, one or more appeals can be allowed for, which can elongate the time it takes to get to a final dispute decision for months, if not years. Thus, in comparison to a public court system, arbitration can be faster and more cost-effective because of less time and resources required over a shorter period.

As a result of these cost and time advantages, within the American legal system, arbitration proceedings have become an increasingly preferred option to resolve disputes regarding domestic and cross-border dealings. Various organizations, such as the International Bar Association, have set broad-based arbitration rules, but many arbitration panels have the option to flexibly modify procedures and rules as deemed necessary and appropriate for the dispute in question. Arbitration is also available for any party, including states, corporations, and individuals, which makes it a viable alternative for actors in the international economic system.

Mediation

Much like arbitration, mediation also involves an impartial third party—referred to as the mediator—to resolve a particular dispute between two or more parties. But unlike an arbitration proceeding, a mediator's decision is often not binding. As a result, a primary objective of a mediation session is often to have a trusted impartial third party to raise the communication lines between the parties to help find common ground to resolve the dispute. Mediation is often used at the early stages in a dispute—even, at times, before arbitration and litigation.

As in arbitration, the relevant parties must also consent to the mediation process. At least one or more of the parties also typically must consent to the mediator(s) chosen to resolve the dispute. Mediators, who are often but not always licensed attorneys and/or judges, are also generally chosen for their expertise and knowledge in a particular field deemed relevant to resolving the dispute. In principle, the mediation process is also open to most actors in the international economic system, including, but not limited to, states, private-sector entities, and individuals.

Negotiation

Another form of alternative dispute resolution is negotiation. Negotiation is the process by which disputes can be resolved and value can be created for the parties involved. As you may imagine, the degrees of formality of negotiations can vary greatly, from a formal negotiation setting in a conference room meeting to a simple e-mail exchange regarding terms and conditions to a particular agreement. At a more conceptual level, two main schools of thought exist relating to negotiations: positional bargaining and principled bargaining.

Positional bargaining occurs when parties' negotiation focuses primarily on each of their respective positions (i.e., set terms and conditions, such as price, quantity, land area, and time), with little or no exploration of the other side's interests (i.e., the rationale underlying one's position). Positional bargaining is often equated to competitive and hard negotiations in which a clear winner or loser is sought.

Positional bargaining often involves some form of haggling or compromise, in which, for example, the price of a particular good is somewhere near the middle point of two extreme price points. For example, you may see positional bargaining at work at a weekend flea market for a used coffee table. The exchange may begin by the buyer offering the seller $10, with a very quick counteroffer of $100. Then comes the negotiation dance in which both sides, if interested, typically begin making concessions toward a price point somewhere near the middle point between $10 and $100.

Here, the negotiator(s) assume a fixed pie (or zero sum game). In this working assumption, the negotiators are in effect engaged in a land grab, whereby one party's gain is directly correlated to the counterparty's loss, similar to a sports competition. Thus, the more points (in the form of price, quantity, land area, time, etc.) gained from the other side, the better it is from a positional negotiator's perspective, because the goal of positional bargaining is to gain as much as possible.

In contrast, principled (or integrative) bargaining involves a different approach. The approach is to not negotiate against the counterparty, but instead, to negotiate with the counterparty (in a form of us instead of you vs. me). In other words, by linking or integrating both sides, opportunities could be sought in a value-added way through various means.

The main school of thought on integrative bargaining is derived from arguably the most popular book related to negotiations, *Getting to Yes*, by Roger Fisher and William Ury of Harvard University's Program on Negotiation. The authors suggest conducting integrative bargaining through the following structured framework of seven elements:

1. Communication (building effective and respectful communication)
2. Relationship (to understand and analyze the type of relationship wanted)
3. Interests (exploring common and shared interests)
4. Options (creating options, or brainstorming, in a form of two heads are better than one)
5. Legitimacy (deciding which options are preferable based on agreed-upon objective criteria)
6. Alternatives (choosing no to an offer based on the calculation that the offer by the counterparty is not better than one's BATNA, which stands for the Best Alternative To a Negotiated Agreement, in essence, one's opportunity cost or best walk-away alternative)
7. Commitment (choosing yes to an offer because it is better than one's BATNA)

In principled negotiations, the spirit is to dig deeper into each party's interests that exist underneath a party's position. This is often done by simply asking "Why?" regarding a particular issue. For example, with the previous coffee table example, the buyer may want to ask why the seller wants $100 for the table. It could be that an underlying reason exists to rationalize the price (e.g., a high quality of wood, historical significance) and vice versa (e.g., the buyer is a student with little cash and just wants basic cheap furniture for his dorm room). The thinking is that exploring each party's underlying interests can sometimes, but not always, help to bridge the gap between differences in a negotiation setting.

Some may ask, "Which negotiation style is better?" Both have their advantages and disadvantages. So rather than giving a broad one-size-fits-all answer, it may be better to analyze the benefits and risks associated with each negotiation style. One advantage of positional bargaining is that it is relatively fast, because only the parties' positions need to be focused on, and furthermore, identifying the positions (e.g., price, quantity, time) of the related parties is fairly easy. One risk is that a relationship is never forged, at least not a sustainable one, because the only point of focus is the parties' positions, not on building a relationship.

Thus, the negotiation can lead to negotiator's remorse, in which either or even both sides are left with a bad taste in their mouth after the negotiation (i.e., the parties do not feel satisfied even after agreement and/or would not be happy having to negotiate with each other again due to a lack of trust or goodwill). Especially in an interconnected and globalized world, in which professionals have only a few degrees of separation, not forging strong relationships can lead to a non-optimal negotiated outcome (i.e., getting to a yes in a deal for the mere sake of reaching an agreement, although the agreement may not substantively be best for the parties). This is often the case because the negotiated outcome is merely a halfway point between two extreme initial positions, whereby both parties fail to fully get what they want.

The advantage of principled (integrative) bargaining is that it focuses more on forging good communication methods to forge a strong relationship whereby creative solutions can result. This approach may lead to a higher chance of reaching a more optimal negotiated outcome. The risk of the principled bargaining strategy is that, because it involves more variables—exploring common interests, creating options together, and seeking legitimate standards—principled negotiations can often take longer to reach a negotiated outcome relative to the more straightforward and simplistic positional bargaining method.

In a more complex negotiation setting, taking more time and effort, the sessions often oscillate between principled and positional bargaining styles, but one takeaway lesson for practitioners and students of negotiation strategy is that more than one method of negotiation strategy can be used to reach your objective.

This section discussed the main alternative dispute resolution strategies and frameworks that exist. The next section focuses on conceptual approaches used by practitioners and others in terms of civil litigation, which often intersects with ADR.

Civil Litigation

What happens when a party is involved in a civil dispute and enters into civil litigation? And what is the litigation process in the event of a civil action lawsuit? The topics of civil action and civil procedure hold some key answers to these and other related questions. Litigation is the legal system's mechanism for resolving disputes between parties. Civil procedure is the body of law that provides the structure and process related to such litigation. Litigation can be initiated by two or more individuals, companies, or other legal persons.

Civil action and procedure's objectives include the following:

- Implementing substantive rules of law and related policy considerations
- Ensuring that the litigation process is fair and transparent
- Seeking an efficient process and outcome

When a lawsuit begins in the litigation process, two main considerations arise: (1) which court, or courts, could have jurisdiction to hear the case; and (2) if more than one court could conceivably have jurisdiction, which specific court would be most beneficial from a legal strategy standpoint for the lawyer's client?

To establish jurisdiction, a court must assert: (1) subject matter jurisdiction over the substantive legal issue; and (2) personal jurisdiction over the relevant parties. Regarding personal jurisdiction, the courts have ruled that the U.S. Constitution requires that, in state courts, the defendant must have "minimum contacts" with the forum state (the state where the lawsuit was filed) in the spirit of fair play and justice. At the federal level, courts often have limited, rather than general, jurisdiction. Thus, in contrast to state courts, federal courts typically have jurisdiction over cases in specific categories.

When can a lawsuit be heard by federal courts? Federal courts generally have jurisdiction over two types of issues:

- Federal questions
- Diversity jurisdiction

Generally, federal questions involve issues such as the Constitution, federal statutes, and federal administrative rules. Diversity jurisdiction typically involves a dispute between parties from two different states. Through diversity jurisdiction, prejudice against out-of-state parties, if heard by a state court instead of a federal court, is prevented. In litigation, the plaintiff can normally choose the court in which to sue. However, the defendant can then ask to remove the case to another court (i.e., from a state to a federal court). When legal issues of two competing jurisdictions exist, an area of law known as conflict of laws arises.

A Brief Overview of a Civil Action Lawsuit: Complaint and Summons

A lawsuit begins with the plaintiff's lawyer drafting and submitting a document known as a complaint. The document "complains" to the court that the defendant violated the plaintiff's legal rights, which links to the facts relevant to the complaint. The complaint also asks the court for a specific remedy for the violation of such legal rights. A summons, which requests the defendant to legally respond to the complaint, is attached to the complaint.

The complaint is also part of the civil action litigation process by:

- Setting forth the basis for jurisdiction
- Putting the defendants on notice that the defendant is being sued, and stating the basis of the lawsuit
- Stipulating the issues of law and fact relevant to the case

Service of process is the next step in the litigation process. Service of process requires that the defendant be "served" a copy of the plaintiff's complaint and summons, delivered by a process server, registered mail, police authority, or other person as required by the court that has jurisdiction in the case.

What legal options exist for the defendant once the plaintiff's complaint has been served to the defendant?

1. *Ignore the plaintiff's complaint.* In a criminal law case, this could lead to the possible arrest of the defendant for failure to appear in court. In a civil law case, the court could rule for a default judgment against the defendant. A default judgment prevents the defendant from then entering any legal defenses in the case.
2. *Raise a legal objection in the form of a motion to dismiss.* In a motion to dismiss, the defendant would argue that, among other things, no remedy exists for the plaintiff's legal claim against the defendant. The motion to dismiss is a formal request to the court by the defendant to dismiss the case without the need to consider the substantive merits of the case.
3. *Dispute the legal sufficiency of the plaintiff's complaint through a demurrer.* Another term for demurrer is a motion to dismiss for failure to state a claim, or failure to state a cause of action.
4. *File an answer to the plaintiff's complaint.* The defendant's answer can include denying, disclaiming, or admitting the plaintiff's allegations, but stating the basis for the defendant's defense in the lawsuit, referred to as an affirmative defense. In an affirmative defense, the defendant argues that even assuming the plaintiff's assertions are true, the defendant's assertions of facts and arguments will prevail over the plaintiff's legal claims.

Discovery Process

How do parties discover the facts in a case? Parties discover the facts in a case through a process called discovery, Discovery is done at the pretrial stage of the lawsuit process.

Discovery methods include the following:

- **Depositions**: Interviews with other parties under oath
- **Interrogatories**: Written questions given to the counterparty
- **Demand for evidence** (motion for production of documents): Related to documents or other physical evidence
- **Physical examination**: Requires the other party to submit to a physical examination when relevant
- **Requests for admissions**: Asks the other party to admit the truth of the facts relevant to the litigation; once the relevant parties believe that certain facts are undisputed, then a request for admission can be issued, narrowing and defining the issues to be tried in the case.

The discovery process helps bring out all of the relevant evidence in a trial to achieve an efficient and transparent process to reach a fair outcome. It also helps the relevant attorneys to better and more clearly define the issues of fact and law in the case. This process enables both sides to bring forth the action and defenses to the case in a more optimal way.

The pretrial phase of the litigation is also an important time to reach a potential out-of-court settlement between the parties. In most U.S. jurisdictions, the majority of cases settle out-of-court before going to trial. Many jurisdictions also have mandatory programs of ADR in the form of arbitration, mediation, or mini-trial. If a pretrial out-of-court settlement cannot be reached between the parties, then the lawsuit moves to the trial phase.

Litigation and Civil Procedure at Trial and Beyond

The trial typically begins with opening statements by both the plaintiff and defendant. The first opening statement is by the plaintiff's legal counsel, because the plaintiff has the burden of proof (under the working assumption of "innocent until proven guilty"). The defendant's opening statement then follows.

The opening statements are followed by production of evidence and arguments pursuant to the rules of evidence of the court's jurisdiction. This can include the calling and examination of witnesses in support of one side of the case. The production of evidentiary proof at trial is governed by the law of civil procedure as well as the law of evidence specific to the court's jurisdiction. Civil procedure controls the order and method of the production of such evidentiary proof. The rules of evidence within civil procedure determine what types of evidence are permissible or not. For example, generally, evidence must be relevant to be admissible in a trial, but exceptions exist, such as when the evidence is harmful character evidence, and if it conflicts with legal policy.

Another example of a rule of evidence is the inadmissibility of hearsay evidence (secondhand testimony or out-of-court statement offered to prove the truth of a statement). For example, a statement such as "I heard John say that Joe (defendant) always drives while he's drunk (intoxicated)" would normally be considered as hearsay evidence, because the person making the statement did not hear the fact directly from Joe, but instead heard it from John, a secondhand testimonial source.

The end of the trial involves closing arguments, which are a summary of each party's case. If the trial is a jury trial, the judge would then instruct the jury on the relevant law. The jury's main task is to make determinations based on issues of fact. Thus, a division of labor exists between the judge (rule of law) and jury (issues of fact) in a jury trial. In a bench trial (a trial without a jury), the judge would consider both issues of law and fact before then rendering a ruling on the case.

The Seventh Amendment to the U.S. Constitution and most state constitutions proclaim the right to a jury trial in civil action cases. Generally, if either party requests a jury trial, then a jury trial will be granted. Similarly, if both parties request a bench trial, then a bench trial is generally granted. In a jury trial, jury members should be representative of the general population and impartial. Thus, if legal counsel for a party can assert that a potential jury or actual jury member is biased, then this issue could be cause for removal of a particular juror.

After the judge and/or jury reaches a verdict, is this the end of the litigation cycle? It generally depends on what the parties are seeking. Among other things, the parties can opt to appeal the case to a higher court. The losing party can appeal (becoming the appellant party), but this is an option, not an obligatory duty. The winning party can also opt to appeal if the party received a partial remedy amount compared to what it expected.

Summary

The vast majority of disputes in the American legal system are settled out-of-court through alternative dispute resolution (ADR) methods before the actual litigation process begins in the courtroom. ADR approaches include mediation, arbitration, and negotiation. The civil litigation process controls the order and method of the production of such evidentiary proof. The rules of evidence within civil procedure determine what types of evidence are permissible. In a civil action lawsuit where civil litigation process applies, the litigation process typically begins with the plaintiff's complaint and summons, which are then served to the defendant. This is followed by various options on how to respond to the plaintiff's complaint and summons, including filing of a motion to dismiss, arguing for affirmative defenses, and even ignoring the complaint and summons, each resulting in various possible subsequent legal responses. If the case reaches the courtroom, various civil litigation procedures can occur, from opening arguments and examination of relevant evidence and testimonies to closing arguments and the rendering of the court's ruling. Such ADR and civil litigation options exist for various related parties to seek legal remedies and justice under the American legal system.

APPENDIX A
HOW THE AMERICAN LEGAL PROCESS WORKS

How Courts Work: The Role and Structure of Courts

Law won't work without independent courts. That means courts that aren't under the thumb of the political powers-that-be. An independent judge can assure that your case will be decided according to the law and the facts—not the vagaries of shifting political currents.

We need courts to interpret and apply the law when parties dispute. In that way, courts take law out of dry and dusty law books, and make it part of the living fabric of our lives. Courts apply the law to specific controversies brought before them. They resolve disputes between people, companies, and units of government.

Often, courts are called on to uphold limitations on the government. They protect against abuses by all branches of government. They protect minorities of all types from the majority, and protect the rights of people who can't protect themselves. They also embody notions of equal treatment and fair play. The courts and the protections of the law are open to everybody.

In any state, there are not one but two distinct court systems: state courts and federal courts. The vast majority of cases—over 95%—are handled by the state courts. The great bulk of legal business—traffic offenses, divorce, wills and estates, buying and selling property—is handled by the state courts, because all these areas are governed primarily by state laws.

Basically, the courts of this country are divided into three layers:

1. Trial courts, where cases start
2. Intermediate (appellate) courts, where most appeals are first heard
3. Courts of last resort (usually called supreme courts), which hear further appeals and have final authority in the cases they hear

The Role of Judges

What does a judge do? Maybe it's best to start with what he or she doesn't do. Even though he or she works for the state, a judge is not a law enforcement officer. A judge is not a prosecutor. Judges don't arrest people or try to prove them guilty.

Judges are like umpires in baseball or referees in football or basketball. Their role is to see that the rules of court procedures are followed by both sides. Like the ump, they call 'em as they see 'em, according to the facts and law—without regard to which side is popular (no home field advantage), without regard to who is "favored," without regard for what the spectators want, and without regard to whether the judge agrees with the law.

The Role of Juries

A jury is a group of people summoned and sworn to decide on the facts at issue in a trial. The jury is composed of people who represent a cross-section of the community. The jury listens to the evidence during a trial, decides what facts the evidence has established, and draws inferences from those facts to form the basis for their decision. The jury decides whether a defendant is "guilty" or "not guilty" in criminal cases, and "liable" or "not liable" in civil cases.

When cases are tried before a jury, the judge still has a major role in determining which evidence may be considered by the jury. The jury is the fact-finder, but it is left to "find" facts only from the evidence which is legally admissible. The judge instructs the jury on the legal principles or rules that must be followed in weighing the facts. If the jury finds the accused guilty or liable, it is up to the judge to sentence the defendant.

Grand Juries

A grand jury is a group of people summoned to determine whether the facts and accusations presented by the prosecutor warrant an indictment and eventual trial of the accused. It is called a grand jury because of the relative large amount of jurors impaneled (traditionally 23) as compared with a petit jury or trial jury.

Grand juries exist in the federal system and in almost all states. However, in only about half the states do grand juries have to be used to bring charges for felonies. In the other states, they may or may not be used to bring charges for felonies—prosecutors have discretion to use them or bring charges on their own.

Grand juries also have a second role in many states: investigating public corruption or undertaking such tasks as monitoring conditions in the jail.

Trial Juries

Trial juries are traditionally composed of 12 members whose verdict is required to be unanimous. Less than unanimous verdicts have been held constitutionally permissible in state, but not federal, criminal proceedings.

Judicial Independence

Before the American Revolution, courts in the colonies were seen as instruments of oppression. Juries could be locked up until they reached the "right" decision. Judges were seen as puppets of the king. In fact, the Declaration of Independence criticized King George III for making "judges dependent upon his will alone for the tenure of their offices and the amount and payment of their salaries."

This experience convinced the founders that Americans needed independent courts to be protected from unreasonable searches, rigged trials, and other examples of overreaching government power. To guarantee rights like freedom of speech and freedom of worship, and make the rule of law a reality, the founders knew that judges had to be servants of law and the Constitution, not the political bosses, not the media, and not special interest groups. The Constitution protected judges from political and public pressure by:

- Specifying that they hold their office "during good behavior." This meant that their appointments are for life.
- Specifying that their salaries cannot be diminished during their tenure. This prevents Congress from retaliating against judges by cutting their pay.
- Making the removal process difficult (only on "impeachment for, and conviction of, treason, bribery, or other high crimes and misdemeanors").

Throughout American history, the independence of the judiciary has protected individual liberties and prevented a tyranny of the majority. Examples include extending voting rights, ending segregation, and protecting the average citizen from unwarranted government intrusion. Emerging democracies look to our system of an independent judiciary as a model. They are all too familiar with the "telephone justice" of dictatorships, in which a judge adjourns court to wait for the call that tells him or her how to decide the case. Judicial independence assures that cases will be decided on their merits. Decisions are based on what is right and just under the law, not what is popular at the moment.

Diagram of How a Case Moves Through the Courts

Civil and Criminal Cases

The law deals with two kinds of cases. Civil cases involve conflicts between people or institutions such as businesses. A civil case usually begins when a person or organization determines that a problem can't be solved without the intervention of the courts. In civil cases, one (or more) of these persons or organizations brings suit (i.e., files a complaint in court that begins a lawsuit).

Criminal cases involve enforcing public codes of behavior as embodied in the laws, with the government prosecuting individuals or institutions. In a criminal case, the government brings charges against the person alleged to have committed the crime.

What types of cases are civil? Divorce and related lawsuits (child support, custody, and the like) account for a very large number of civil cases. Cases involving contracts are also frequent. Automobile collisions account for many tort (personal injury) cases, another common kind of civil case. An auto collision gives rise to a civil case if one driver sues the other, or if a passenger in one of the cars sues either driver. An auto collision might also lead to a criminal case, if it involves allegations of a crime such as drunken driving or leaving the scene of an accident.

In many parts of the world, civil and criminal legal actions are combined into one case, but in our country they are not. If there are serious civil and criminal aspects of an event, there will be two (or more) distinct cases. An example would be a crime leading to a criminal trial of the defendant, with the victims filing a separate civil suit against the defendant to recover damages caused by the crime.

Jurisdiction and Venue

The plaintiff's lawyer must decide where to file the case. A court has no authority to decide a case unless it has jurisdiction over the person or property involved. To have jurisdiction, a court must have authority over the subject matter of the case and the court must be able to exercise control over the defendant, or the property involved must be located in the area under the court's control. The extent of the court's control over persons and property is set by law.

Certain actions are transitory. They can be brought wherever the defendant may be found and served with a summons, and where the jurisdiction has sufficient contact with one of the parties and the incident that gave rise to the suit. An example would be a lawsuit against a business—it would probably be sufficient to file suit in any county in which the business has an operation, and not necessary to file suit in the county where it is headquartered. Other actions—such as foreclosing on a piece of property—are local. They can be brought only in the county where the subject of the suit is located.

Venue refers to the county or district within a state or the U.S. where the lawsuit is to be tried. The venue of a lawsuit is set by statute, but it can sometimes be changed to another county or district. For example, if a case has received widespread pre-trial publicity, one of the parties may make a motion (request to the judge) for change of venue in an effort to secure jurors who haven't already formed an opinion about the case. Venue also may be changed for the convenience of witnesses.

Pleadings

A lawsuit begins when the person bringing the suit files a complaint. This first step begins what is known as the pleadings stage of the suit. Pleadings are certain formal documents filed with the court that state the parties' basic positions.

Common pre-trial pleadings include:

- **Complaint** (or petition or bill). Probably the most important pleading in a civil case, since by setting out the plaintiff's version of the facts and specifying the damages, it frames the issues of the case. It includes various counts—that is, distinct statements of the plaintiff's cause of action—highlighting the factual and legal basis of the suit.
- **Answer**. This statement by the defendant usually explains why the plaintiff should not prevail. It may also offer additional facts, or plead an excuse.
- **Reply**. Any party in the case may have to file a reply, which is an answer to new allegations raised in pleadings.
- **Counterclaim**. The defendant may file a counterclaim, which asserts that the plaintiff has injured the defendant in some way, and should pay damages. ("You're suing me? Well then, I'm suing you.") It may be filed separately or as part of the answer. If a counterclaim is filed, the plaintiff must be given the opportunity to respond by filing a reply.

Motions

Motions are not pleadings but are requests for the judge to make a legal ruling. Some of the most common pre-trial motions include:

- **Motion to Discover**. A motion by which one party seeks to gain information from the adverse party.
- **Motion to Dismiss**. This motion asks the court to dismiss the suit because the suit doesn't have a legally sound basis, even if all the facts alleged are proven true.
- **Motion for Summary Judgment** (sometimes called motion for summary disposition). This motion asks the court for a judgment on the merits of the case before the trial. It is properly made where there is no dispute about the facts and only a question of law needs to be decided.

Discovery

To begin preparing for trial, both sides engage in discovery. This is the formal process of exchanging information between the parties about the witnesses and evidence they'll present at trial. Discovery enables the parties to know before the trial begins what evidence may be presented. It's designed to prevent "trial by ambush," where one side doesn't learn of the other side's evidence or witnesses until the trial, when there's no time to obtain answering evidence.

One of the most common methods of discovery is to take depositions. A deposition is an out-of-court statement given under oath by any person involved in the case. It is to be used at trial or in preparation for trial. It may be in the form of a written transcript, a videotape, or both. In most states, either of the parties may take the deposition of the other party, or of any other witness. Both sides have the right to be present during oral depositions.

Depositions enable a party to know in advance what a witness will say at the trial. Depositions can also be taken to obtain the testimony of important witnesses who can't appear during the trial. In that case, they're read into evidence at the trial. Often a witness's deposition will be taken by the opposing side and used to discredit the witness's testimony at trial if the trial testimony varies from the testimony taken during the deposition. (A lawyer might ask a witness at trial, "Are you lying now or were you lying then?")

Usually depositions consist of an oral examination, followed by cross-examination by the opposing side. In addition to taking depositions, either party may submit written questions, called interrogatories, to the other party and require that they be answered in writing under oath. If one party chooses to use an interrogatory, written questions are sent to the lawyer representing the other side, and that party has a period of time in which to answer.

Other methods of discovery include subpoenaing or requiring the other side to produce books, records, or other documents for inspection (a subpoena is a written order issued by a court compelling a person to testify or produce certain physical evidence such as records); having the other side submit to a physical examination; or asking that a document be submitted for examination to determine if it is genuine.

Opening Statements

The purpose of opening statements by each side is to tell jurors something about the case they will be hearing. The opening statements must be confined to facts that will be proved by the evidence, and cannot be argumentative.

The trial begins with the opening statement of the party with the burden of proof. This is the party that brought the case to court—the government in a criminal prosecution or the plaintiff in a civil case—and has to prove its case in order to prevail. The defense lawyer follows with his or her opening statement. In some states, the defense may reserve its opening statement until the end of the plaintiff's or government's case. Either lawyer may choose not to present an opening statement.

In a criminal trial, the burden of proof rests with the government, which must prove beyond a reasonable doubt that the defendant is guilty. The defendant does not need to prove his or her innocence—the burden is on the government. In a civil trial, the plaintiff has the burden of proof, and generally must prove liability by a preponderance of the evidence (i.e., the greater weight of the evidence). The degree of proof required in a civil case is far less stringent than in a criminal case. Once again, the defendant does not have to prove that he or she is not liable.

Evidence

The heart of the case is the presentation of evidence. There are two types of evidence—direct and circumstantial:

- Direct evidence usually is that which speaks for itself: eyewitness accounts, a confession, or a weapon.
- Circumstantial evidence usually is that which suggests a fact by implication or inference: the appearance of the scene of a crime, testimony that suggests a connection or link with a crime, physical evidence that suggests criminal activity.

Both kinds of evidence are a part of most trials, with circumstantial evidence probably being used more often than direct. Either kind of evidence can be offered in oral testimony of witnesses or physical exhibits, including fingerprints, test results, and documents. Neither kind of evidence is more valuable than the other.

Strict rules govern the kinds of evidence that may be admitted into a trial, and the presentation of evidence is governed by formal rules.

Closing Arguments

The lawyers' closing arguments or summations discuss the evidence and properly drawn inferences. The lawyers cannot talk about issues outside the case or about evidence that was not presented. The judge usually indicates to the lawyers before closing arguments begin which instructions he or she intends to give the jury. In their closing arguments the lawyers can comment on the jury instructions and relate them to the evidence.

The lawyer for the plaintiff or government usually goes first. The lawyer sums up and comments on the evidence in the most favorable light for his or her side, showing how it proved what he or she had to prove to prevail in the case. After that side has made its case, the defense then presents its closing arguments. The defense lawyer usually answers statements made in the plaintiff's or government's argument, points out defects in their case and sums up the facts favorable to his or her client.

Because the plaintiff or government has the burden of proof, the lawyer for that side is then entitled to make a concluding argument, sometimes called a rebuttal. This is a chance to respond to the defendant's points and make one final appeal to the jury. Occasionally the defense may choose not to make a closing statement. If so, the plaintiff or government loses the right to make a second argument.

Verdict

After reaching a decision, the jury notifies the bailiff, who notifies the judge. All of the participants reconvene in the courtroom and the decision is announced. The announcement may be made by either the foreperson or the court clerk.

Possible verdicts in criminal cases are "guilty" or "not guilty." In a civil suit, the jury will find for the plaintiff or the defendant. If the jury finds for the plaintiff, it will also usually set out the amount the defendant should pay the plaintiff for damages, often after a separate hearing concerning damages. The jury will also make a decision on any counterclaims that may be part of the case.

The lawyer for either party may ask that the jury be polled, although the request usually comes from the losing party. This means each juror will be asked if he or she agrees with the decision, as announced. This is to make sure that the verdict announced is the actual verdict of the jury. After the decision is read and accepted by the court, the jury is dismissed, and the trial is over.

Judgment

The decision of the jury doesn't take effect until the judge enters a judgment on the decision—that is, an order that it be filed in public records.

In a civil suit, the judge may have the authority to increase or decrease the amount of damages awarded by the jury, or to make some other modifications before entering judgment. In criminal cases, the judge generally has no authority to modify the verdict. In most jurisdictions, he or she must accept it or reject it (e.g., by granting a motion in arrest of judgment).

If the defendant doesn't pay the damages awarded to the plaintiff in a civil case, the plaintiff may ask for an execution of the judgment. The clerk of the court in such a case will deliver the execution to the sheriff, commanding him to take and sell the property of the defendant and apply that money to the amount of the judgment.

Sentencing

If the defendant is convicted in a criminal case, the judge will set a date for sentencing. Before that time, a pre-sentence investigation will take place to help the judge determine the appropriate sentence from the range of possible sentences set out in the statutes. The pre-sentence investigation may consider the defendant's prior criminal record, family situation, health, work record, and any other relevant factor.

In most states and in the federal courts, only the judge determines the sentence to be imposed. (The main exception is that in most states juries impose sentence in cases where the death penalty is a possibility.) The federal courts and some states have sentencing guidelines to guide judges in determining appropriate sentences and to encourage uniformity.

Appeals

A popular misconception is that cases are always appealed. Not often does a losing party have an automatic right of appeal. There usually must be a legal basis for the appeal—an alleged material error in the trial—not just the fact that the losing party didn't like the verdict.

In a civil case, either party may appeal to a higher court. In a criminal case, only the defendant has a right to an appeal in most states. (Some states give the prosecution a limited right to appeal to determine certain points of law. These appeals usually occur before the actual trial begins. Appeals by the prosecution after a verdict are not normally allowed because of the prohibition in the U. S. Constitution against double jeopardy, or being tried twice for the same crime.)

Criminal defendants convicted in state courts have a further safeguard. After using all of their rights of appeal on the state level, they may file a writ of habeas corpus in the federal courts in an attempt to show that their federal constitutional rights were violated. The right of a federal review imposes the check of the federal courts on abuses that may occur in the state courts.

An appeal is not a retrial or a new trial of the case. The appeals courts do not usually consider new witnesses or new evidence. Appeals in either civil or criminal cases are usually based on arguments that there were errors in the trial's procedure or errors in the judge's interpretation of the law.

Appeal Procedure

The party appealing is called the appellant, or sometimes the petitioner. The other party is the appellee or the respondent. The appeal is instituted with the filing of a notice of appeal. This filing marks the beginning of the time period within which the appellant must file a brief, a written argument containing that side's view of the facts and the legal arguments upon which they rely in seeking a reversal of the trial court. The appellee then has a specified time to file an answering brief. The appellant may then file a second brief answering the appellee's brief.

Sometimes, appeals courts make their decision only on the basis of the written briefs. Sometimes, they hear oral arguments before deciding a case. Often the court will ask that the case be set for oral argument, or one of the parties will request oral argument. At oral argument, each side's attorney is given a relatively brief opportunity to argue the case to the court, and to answer questions posed by the judges. In the U.S. Supreme Court, for example, an hour is set for oral argument of most cases, which gives each side's lawyers about half an hour to make their oral argument and answer questions. In the federal courts of appeals, the attorneys are often allotted less time than that—10- or 15-minute arguments are common.

The appellate court determines whether errors occurred in applying the law at the lower court level. It generally will reverse a trial court only for an error of law. Not every error of law, however, is cause for a reversal. Some are harmless errors that did not prejudice the rights of the parties to a fair trial. For example, in a criminal case a higher court may conclude that the trial judge gave a legally improper instruction to the jury, but if the mistake were minor and in the opinion of the appellate court had no bearing on the jury's finding, the appellate court may hold it a harmless error and let a guilty verdict stand. However, an error of law, such as admitting improper evidence, may be determined to be a harmful and therefore reversible error.

After a case is orally argued or otherwise presented for judgment, the appeals court judges will meet in conference to discuss the case. Appellate courts often issue written decisions, particularly when the decision deals with a new interpretation of the law, establishes a new precedent, etc. At the conference, one judge will be designated to write an opinion. The opinion may go through several drafts before a majority of the court agrees with it. Judges disagreeing with the majority opinion may issue a dissenting opinion. Judges agreeing with the result of a majority decision but disagreeing with the majority's reasoning may file a concurring opinion. Occasionally the appeals court will simply issue an unsigned opinion. These are called per curiam (by the court).

If the appeals court affirms the lower court's judgment, the case ends, unless the losing party appeals to a higher court. The lower court decision also stands if the appeals court simply dismisses the appeal (usually for reasons of jurisdiction).

If the judgment is reversed, the appellate court will usually send the case back to a lower court (remand it) and order the trial court to take further action. It may order that:

- A new trial be held.
- The trial court's judgment be modified or corrected.
- The trial court reconsider the facts, take additional evidence, or consider the case in light of a recent decision by the appellate court.

In a civil case, an appeal doesn't ordinarily prevent the enforcement of the trial court's judgment. The winning party in the trial court may order the judgment executed. However, the appealing party can file an appeal or supersede as bond. The filing of this bond will prevent, or stay, further action on the judgment until the appeal is over by guaranteeing that the appealing party will pay or perform the judgment if it is not reversed on appeal.

Source: ABA website, http://www.americanbar.org/groups/public_education/resources/law_related_education_network/how_courts_work/court_role.html (last visited September 12, 2014).

APPENDIX B
U.S. CONSTITUTION AND BILL OF RIGHTS

The Constitution of the United States: A Transcription

Note: The following text is a transcription of the Constitution in its original form. Items that are underlined have since been amended or superseded.

We the People of the United States, in Order to form a more perfect Union, establish Justice, insure domestic Tranquility, provide for the common defence, promote the general Welfare, and secure the Blessings of Liberty to ourselves and our Posterity, do ordain and establish this Constitution for the United States of America.

Article. I.

Section. 1.

All legislative Powers herein granted shall be vested in a Congress of the United States, which shall consist of a Senate and House of Representatives.

Section. 2.

The House of Representatives shall be composed of Members chosen every second Year by the People of the several States, and the Electors in each State shall have the Qualifications requisite for Electors of the most numerous Branch of the State Legislature.

No Person shall be a Representative who shall not have attained to the Age of twenty five Years, and been seven Years a Citizen of the United States, and who shall not, when elected, be an Inhabitant of that State in which he shall be chosen.

Representatives and direct Taxes shall be apportioned among the several States which may be included within this Union, according to their respective Numbers, which shall be determined by adding to the whole Number of free Persons, including those bound to Service for a Term of Years, and excluding Indians not taxed, three fifths of all other Persons. The actual Enumeration shall be made within three Years after the first Meeting of the Congress of the United States, and within every subsequent Term of ten Years, in such Manner as they shall by Law direct. The Number of Representatives shall not exceed one for every thirty Thousand, but each State shall have at Least one Representative; and until such enumeration shall be made, the State of New Hampshire shall be entitled to chuse three, Massachusetts eight, Rhode-Island and Providence Plantations one, Connecticut five, New-York six, New Jersey four, Pennsylvania eight, Delaware one, Maryland six, Virginia ten, North Carolina five, South Carolina five, and Georgia three.

When vacancies happen in the Representation from any State, the Executive Authority thereof shall issue Writs of Election to fill such Vacancies.

The House of Representatives shall chuse their Speaker and other Officers; and shall have the sole Power of Impeachment.

Section. 3.

The Senate of the United States shall be composed of two Senators from each State, chosen by the Legislature thereof for six Years; and each Senator shall have one Vote.

Immediately after they shall be assembled in Consequence of the first Election, they shall be divided as equally as may be into three Classes. The Seats of the Senators of the first Class shall be vacated at the Expiration of the second Year, of the second Class at the Expiration of the fourth Year, and of the third Class at the Expiration of the sixth Year, so that one third may be chosen every second Year; and if Vacancies happen by Resignation, or otherwise, during the Recess of the Legislature of any State, the Executive thereof may make temporary Appointments until the next Meeting of the Legislature, which shall then fill such Vacancies.

No Person shall be a Senator who shall not have attained to the Age of thirty Years, and been nine Years a Citizen of the United States, and who shall not, when elected, be an Inhabitant of that State for which he shall be chosen.

The Vice President of the United States shall be President of the Senate, but shall have no Vote, unless they be equally divided.

The Senate shall chuse their other Officers, and also a President pro tempore, in the Absence of the Vice President, or when he shall exercise the Office of President of the United States.

The Senate shall have the sole Power to try all Impeachments. When sitting for that Purpose, they shall be on Oath or Affirmation. When the President of the United States is tried, the Chief Justice shall preside: And no Person shall be convicted without the Concurrence of two thirds of the Members present.

Judgment in Cases of Impeachment shall not extend further than to removal from Office, and disqualification to hold and enjoy any Office of honor, Trust or Profit under the United States: but the Party convicted shall nevertheless be liable and subject to Indictment, Trial, Judgment and Punishment, according to Law.

Section. 4.

The Times, Places and Manner of holding Elections for Senators and Representatives, shall be prescribed in each State by the Legislature thereof; but the Congress may at any time by Law make or alter such Regulations, except as to the Places of chusing Senators.

The Congress shall assemble at least once in every Year, and such Meeting shall be on the first Monday in December, unless they shall by Law appoint a different Day.

Section. 5.

Each House shall be the Judge of the Elections, Returns and Qualifications of its own Members, and a Majority of each shall constitute a Quorum to do Business; but a smaller Number may adjourn from day to day, and may be authorized to compel the Attendance of absent Members, in such Manner, and under such Penalties as each House may provide.

Each House may determine the Rules of its Proceedings, punish its Members for disorderly Behaviour, and, with the Concurrence of two thirds, expel a Member.

Each House shall keep a Journal of its Proceedings, and from time to time publish the same, excepting such Parts as may in their Judgment require Secrecy; and the Yeas and Nays of the Members of either House on any question shall, at the Desire of one fifth of those Present, be entered on the Journal.

Neither House, during the Session of Congress, shall, without the Consent of the other, adjourn for more than three days, nor to any other Place than that in which the two Houses shall be sitting.

Section. 6.

The Senators and Representatives shall receive a Compensation for their Services, to be ascertained by Law, and paid out of the Treasury of the United States. They shall in all Cases, except Treason, Felony and Breach of the Peace, be privileged from Arrest during their Attendance at the Session of their respective Houses, and in going to and returning from the same; and for any Speech or Debate in either House, they shall not be questioned in any other Place.

No Senator or Representative shall, during the Time for which he was elected, be appointed to any civil Office under the Authority of the United States, which shall have been created, or the Emoluments whereof shall have been encreased during such time; and no Person holding any Office under the United States, shall be a Member of either House during his Continuance in Office.

Section. 7.

All Bills for raising Revenue shall originate in the House of Representatives; but the Senate may propose or concur with Amendments as on other Bills.

Every Bill which shall have passed the House of Representatives and the Senate, shall, before it become a Law, be presented to the President of the United States: If he approve he shall sign it, but if not he shall return it, with his Objections to that House in which it shall have originated, who shall enter the Objections at large on their Journal, and proceed to reconsider it. If after such Reconsideration two thirds of that House shall agree to pass the Bill, it shall be sent, together with the Objections, to the other House, by which it shall likewise be reconsidered, and if approved by two thirds of that House, it shall become a Law. But in all such Cases the Votes of both Houses shall be determined by yeas and Nays, and the Names of the Persons voting for and against the Bill shall be entered on the Journal of each House respectively. If any Bill shall not be returned by the President within ten Days (Sundays excepted) after it shall have been presented to him, the Same shall be a Law, in like Manner as if he had signed it, unless the Congress by their Adjournment prevent its Return, in which Case it shall not be a Law.

Every Order, Resolution, or Vote to which the Concurrence of the Senate and House of Representatives may be necessary (except on a question of Adjournment) shall be presented to the President of the United States; and before the Same shall take Effect, shall be approved by him, or being disapproved by him, shall be repassed by two thirds of the Senate and House of Representatives, according to the Rules and Limitations prescribed in the Case of a Bill.

Section. 8.

The Congress shall have Power

To lay and collect Taxes, Duties, Imposts and Excises, to pay the Debts and provide for the common Defence and general Welfare of the United States; but all Duties, Imposts and Excises shall be uniform throughout the United States;

To borrow Money on the credit of the United States;

To regulate Commerce with foreign Nations, and among the several States, and with the Indian Tribes;

To establish an uniform Rule of Naturalization, and uniform Laws on the subject of Bankruptcies throughout the United States;

To coin Money, regulate the Value thereof, and of foreign Coin, and fix the Standard of Weights and Measures;

To provide for the Punishment of counterfeiting the Securities and current Coin of the United States;

To establish Post Offices and post Roads;

To promote the Progress of Science and useful Arts, by securing for limited Times to Authors and Inventors the exclusive Right to their respective Writings and Discoveries;

To constitute Tribunals inferior to the supreme Court;

To define and punish Piracies and Felonies committed on the high Seas, and Offences against the Law of Nations;

To declare War, grant Letters of Marque and Reprisal, and make Rules concerning Captures on Land and Water;

To raise and support Armies, but no Appropriation of Money to that Use shall be for a longer Term than two Years;

To provide and maintain a Navy;

To make Rules for the Government and Regulation of the land and naval Forces;

To provide for calling forth the Militia to execute the Laws of the Union, suppress Insurrections and repel Invasions;

To provide for organizing, arming, and disciplining, the Militia, and for governing such Part of them as may be employed in the Service of the United States, reserving to the States respectively, the Appointment of the Officers, and the Authority of training the Militia according to the discipline prescribed by Congress;

To exercise exclusive Legislation in all Cases whatsoever, over such District (not exceeding ten Miles square) as may, by Cession of particular States, and the Acceptance of Congress, become the Seat of the Government of the United States, and to exercise like Authority over all Places purchased by the Consent of the Legislature of the State in which the Same shall be, for the Erection of Forts, Magazines, Arsenals, dock-Yards, and other needful Buildings;—And

To make all Laws which shall be necessary and proper for carrying into Execution the foregoing Powers, and all other Powers vested by this Constitution in the Government of the United States, or in any Department or Officer thereof.

Section. 9.

The Migration or Importation of such Persons as any of the States now existing shall think proper to admit, shall not be prohibited by the Congress prior to the Year one thousand eight hundred and eight, but a Tax or duty may be imposed on such Importation, not exceeding ten dollars for each Person.

The Privilege of the Writ of Habeas Corpus shall not be suspended, unless when in Cases of Rebellion or Invasion the public Safety may require it.

No Bill of Attainder or ex post facto Law shall be passed.

No Capitation, or other direct, Tax shall be laid, unless in Proportion to the Census or enumeration herein before directed to be taken.

No Tax or Duty shall be laid on Articles exported from any State.

No Preference shall be given by any Regulation of Commerce or Revenue to the Ports of one State over those of another; nor shall Vessels bound to, or from, one State, be obliged to enter, clear, or pay Duties in another.

No Money shall be drawn from the Treasury, but in Consequence of Appropriations made by Law; and a regular Statement and Account of the Receipts and Expenditures of all public Money shall be published from time to time.

No Title of Nobility shall be granted by the United States: And no Person holding any Office of Profit or Trust under them, shall, without the Consent of the Congress, accept of any present, Emolument, Office, or Title, of any kind whatever, from any King, Prince, or foreign State.

Section. 10.

No State shall enter into any Treaty, Alliance, or Confederation; grant Letters of Marque and Reprisal; coin Money; emit Bills of Credit; make any Thing but gold and silver Coin a Tender in Payment of Debts; pass any Bill of Attainder, ex post facto Law, or Law impairing the Obligation of Contracts, or grant any Title of Nobility.

No State shall, without the Consent of the Congress, lay any Imposts or Duties on Imports or Exports, except what may be absolutely necessary for executing it's inspection Laws: and the net Produce of all Duties and Imposts, laid by any State on Imports or Exports, shall be for the Use of the Treasury of the United States; and all such Laws shall be subject to the Revision and Controul of the Congress.

No State shall, without the Consent of Congress, lay any Duty of Tonnage, keep Troops, or Ships of War in time of Peace, enter into any Agreement or Compact with another State, or with a foreign Power, or engage in War, unless actually invaded, or in such imminent Danger as will not admit of delay.

Article. II.

Section. 1.

The executive Power shall be vested in a President of the United States of America. He shall hold his Office during the Term of four Years, and, together with the Vice President, chosen for the same Term, be elected, as follows:

Each State shall appoint, in such Manner as the Legislature thereof may direct, a Number of Electors, equal to the whole Number of Senators and Representatives to which the State may be entitled in the Congress: but no Senator or Representative, or Person holding an Office of Trust or Profit under the United States, shall be appointed an Elector.

The Electors shall meet in their respective States, and vote by Ballot for two Persons, of whom one at least shall not be an Inhabitant of the same State with themselves. And they shall make a List of all the Persons voted for, and of the Number of Votes for each; which List they shall sign and certify, and transmit sealed to the Seat of the Government of the United States, directed to the President of the Senate. The President of the Senate shall, in the Presence of the Senate and House of Representatives, open all the Certificates, and the Votes shall then be counted. The Person having the greatest Number of Votes shall be the President, if such Number be a Majority of the whole Number of Electors appointed; and if there be more than one who have such Majority, and have an equal Number of Votes, then the House of Representatives shall immediately chuse by Ballot one of them for President; and if no Person have a Majority, then from the five highest on the List the said House shall in like Manner chuse the President. But in chusing the President, the Votes shall be taken by States, the Representation from each State having one Vote; A quorum for this purpose shall consist of a Member or Members from two thirds of the States, and a Majority of all the States shall be necessary to a Choice. In every Case, after the Choice of the President, the Person having the greatest Number of Votes of the Electors shall be the Vice President. But if there should remain two or more who have equal Votes, the Senate shall chuse from them by Ballot the Vice President.

The Congress may determine the Time of chusing the Electors, and the Day on which they shall give their Votes; which Day shall be the same throughout the United States.

No Person except a natural born Citizen, or a Citizen of the United States, at the time of the Adoption of this Constitution, shall be eligible to the Office of President; neither shall any Person be eligible to that Office who shall not have attained to the Age of thirty five Years, and been fourteen Years a Resident within the United States.

In Case of the Removal of the President from Office, or of his Death, Resignation, or Inability to discharge the Powers and Duties of the said Office, the Same shall devolve on the Vice President, and the Congress may by Law provide for the Case of Removal, Death, Resignation or Inability, both of the President and Vice President, declaring what Officer shall then act as President, and such Officer shall act accordingly, until the Disability be removed, or a President shall be elected.

The President shall, at stated Times, receive for his Services, a Compensation, which shall neither be increased nor diminished during the Period for which he shall have been elected, and he shall not receive within that Period any other Emolument from the United States, or any of them.

Before he enter on the Execution of his Office, he shall take the following Oath or Affirmation:—"I do solemnly swear (or affirm) that I will faithfully execute the Office of President of the United States, and will to the best of my Ability, preserve, protect and defend the Constitution of the United States."

Section. 2.

The President shall be Commander in Chief of the Army and Navy of the United States, and of the Militia of the several States, when called into the actual Service of the United States; he may require the Opinion, in writing, of the principal Officer in each of the executive Departments, upon any Subject relating to the Duties of their respective Offices, and he shall have Power to grant Reprieves and Pardons for Offences against the United States, except in Cases of Impeachment.

He shall have Power, by and with the Advice and Consent of the Senate, to make Treaties, provided two thirds of the Senators present concur; and he shall nominate, and by and with the Advice and Consent of the Senate, shall appoint Ambassadors, other public Ministers and Consuls, Judges of the supreme Court, and all other Officers of the United States, whose Appointments are not herein otherwise provided for, and which shall be established by Law: but the Congress may by Law vest the Appointment of such inferior Officers, as they think proper, in the President alone, in the Courts of Law, or in the Heads of Departments.

The President shall have Power to fill up all Vacancies that may happen during the Recess of the Senate, by granting Commissions which shall expire at the End of their next Session.

Section. 3.

He shall from time to time give to the Congress Information of the State of the Union, and recommend to their Consideration such Measures as he shall judge necessary and expedient; he may, on extraordinary Occasions, convene both Houses, or either of them, and in Case of Disagreement between them, with Respect to the Time of Adjournment, he may adjourn them to such Time as he shall think proper; he shall receive Ambassadors and other public Ministers; he shall take Care that the Laws be faithfully executed, and shall Commission all the Officers of the United States.

Section. 4.

The President, Vice President and all civil Officers of the United States, shall be removed from Office on Impeachment for, and Conviction of, Treason, Bribery, or other high Crimes and Misdemeanors.

Article. III.

Section. 1.

The judicial Power of the United States shall be vested in one supreme Court, and in such inferior Courts as the Congress may from time to time ordain and establish. The Judges, both of the supreme and inferior Courts, shall hold their Offices during good Behaviour, and shall, at stated Times, receive for their Services a Compensation, which shall not be diminished during their Continuance in Office.

Section. 2.

The judicial Power shall extend to all Cases, in Law and Equity, arising under this Constitution, the Laws of the United States, and Treaties made, or which shall be made, under their Authority;—to all Cases affecting Ambassadors, other public Ministers and Consuls;—to all Cases of admiralty and maritime Jurisdiction;—to Controversies to which the United States shall be a Party;—to Controversies between two or more States;—between a State and Citizens of another State,—between Citizens of different States,—between Citizens of the same State claiming Lands under Grants of different States, and between a State, or the Citizens thereof, and foreign States, Citizens or Subjects.

In all Cases affecting Ambassadors, other public Ministers and Consuls, and those in which a State shall be Party, the supreme Court shall have original Jurisdiction. In all the other Cases before mentioned, the supreme Court shall have appellate Jurisdiction, both as to Law and Fact, with such Exceptions, and under such Regulations as the Congress shall make.

The Trial of all Crimes, except in Cases of Impeachment, shall be by Jury; and such Trial shall be held in the State where the said Crimes shall have been committed; but when not committed within any State, the Trial shall be at such Place or Places as the Congress may by Law have directed.

Section. 3.

Treason against the United States, shall consist only in levying War against them, or in adhering to their Enemies, giving them Aid and Comfort. No Person shall be convicted of Treason unless on the Testimony of two Witnesses to the same overt Act, or on Confession in open Court.

The Congress shall have Power to declare the Punishment of Treason, but no Attainder of Treason shall work Corruption of Blood, or Forfeiture except during the Life of the Person attainted.

Article. IV.

Section. 1.

Full Faith and Credit shall be given in each State to the public Acts, Records, and judicial Proceedings of every other State. And the Congress may by general Laws prescribe the Manner in which such Acts, Records and Proceedings shall be proved, and the Effect thereof.

Section. 2.

The Citizens of each State shall be entitled to all Privileges and Immunities of Citizens in the several States.

A Person charged in any State with Treason, Felony, or other Crime, who shall flee from Justice, and be found in another State, shall on Demand of the executive Authority of the State from which he fled, be delivered up, to be removed to the State having Jurisdiction of the Crime.

No Person held to Service or Labour in one State, under the Laws thereof, escaping into another, shall, in Consequence of any Law or Regulation therein, be discharged from such Service or Labour, but shall be delivered up on Claim of the Party to whom such Service or Labour may be due.

Section. 3.

New States may be admitted by the Congress into this Union; but no new State shall be formed or erected within the Jurisdiction of any other State; nor any State be formed by the Junction of two or more States, or Parts of States, without the Consent of the Legislatures of the States concerned as well as of the Congress.

The Congress shall have Power to dispose of and make all needful Rules and Regulations respecting the Territory or other Property belonging to the United States; and nothing in this Constitution shall be so construed as to Prejudice any Claims of the United States, or of any particular State.

Section. 4.

The United States shall guarantee to every State in this Union a Republican Form of Government, and shall protect each of them against Invasion; and on Application of the Legislature, or of the Executive (when the Legislature cannot be convened), against domestic Violence.

Article. V.

The Congress, whenever two thirds of both Houses shall deem it necessary, shall propose Amendments to this Constitution, or, on the Application of the Legislatures of two thirds of the several States, shall call a Convention for proposing Amendments, which, in either Case, shall be valid to all Intents and Purposes, as Part of this Constitution, when ratified by the Legislatures of three fourths of the several States, or by Conventions in three fourths thereof, as the one or the other Mode of Ratification may be proposed by the Congress; Provided that no Amendment which may be made prior to the Year One thousand eight hundred and eight shall in any Manner affect the first and fourth Clauses in the Ninth Section of the first Article; and that no State, without its Consent, shall be deprived of its equal Suffrage in the Senate.

Article. VI.

All Debts contracted and Engagements entered into, before the Adoption of this Constitution, shall be as valid against the United States under this Constitution, as under the Confederation.

This Constitution, and the Laws of the United States which shall be made in Pursuance thereof; and all Treaties made, or which shall be made, under the Authority of the

United States, shall be the supreme Law of the Land; and the Judges in every State shall be bound thereby, any Thing in the Constitution or Laws of any State to the Contrary notwithstanding.

The Senators and Representatives before mentioned, and the Members of the several State Legislatures, and all executive and judicial Officers, both of the United States and of the several States, shall be bound by Oath or Affirmation, to support this Constitution; but no religious Test shall ever be required as a Qualification to any Office or public Trust under the United States.

Article. VII.

The Ratification of the Conventions of nine States, shall be sufficient for the Establishment of this Constitution between the States so ratifying the Same.

The Word, "the," being interlined between the seventh and eighth Lines of the first Page, the Word "Thirty" being partly written on an Erazure in the fifteenth Line of the first Page, The Words "is tried" being interlined between the thirty second and thirty third Lines of the first Page and the Word "the" being interlined between the forty third and forty fourth Lines of the second Page.

Attest William Jackson Secretary

done in Convention by the Unanimous Consent of the States present the Seventeenth Day of September in the Year of our Lord one thousand seven hundred and Eighty seven and of the Independance of the United States of America the Twelfth In witness whereof We have hereunto subscribed our Names,

G. Washington Presidt and deputy from Virginia

Delaware *Geo: Read Gunning Bedford jun*

John Dickinson

Richard Bassett

Jaco: Broom

Maryland

James McHenry

Dan of St Thos. Jenifer

Danl. Carroll

Virginia

John Blair

James Madison Jr.

North Carolina

Wm. Blount

Richd. Dobbs Spaight

Hu Williamson

South Carolina

J. Rutledge

Charles Cotesworth Pinckney

Charles Pinckney

Pierce Butler

Georgia

William Few

Abr Baldwin

New Hampshire

John Langdon

Nicholas Gilman

Massachusetts

Nathaniel Gorham

Rufus King

Connecticut

Wm. Saml. Johnson

Roger Sherman

New York

Alexander Hamilton

New Jersey

Wil: Livingston

David Brearley

Wm. Paterson

Jona: Dayton

Pennsylvania

B Franklin

Thomas Mifflin

Robt. Morris

Geo. Clymer

Thos. FitzSimons

Jared Ingersoll

James Wilson

Gouv Morris

The Bill of Rights: A Transcription

The Preamble to The Bill of Rights

Congress of the United States

begun and held at the City of New-York, on

Wednesday the fourth of March, one thousand seven hundred and eighty nine.

THE Conventions of a number of the States, having at the time of their adopting the Constitution, expressed a desire, in order to prevent misconstruction or abuse of its powers, that further declaratory and restrictive clauses should be added: And as extending the ground of public confidence in the Government, will best ensure the beneficent ends of its institution.

RESOLVED by the Senate and House of Representatives of the United States of America, in Congress assembled, two thirds of both Houses concurring, that the following Articles be proposed to the Legislatures of the several States, as amendments to the Constitution of the United States, all, or any of which Articles, when ratified by three fourths of the said Legislatures, to be valid to all intents and purposes, as part of the said Constitution; viz.

ARTICLES in addition to, and Amendment of the Constitution of the United States of America, proposed by Congress, and ratified by the Legislatures of the several States, pursuant to the fifth Article of the original Constitution.

Note: The following text is a transcription of the first ten amendments to the Constitution in their original form. These amendments were ratified December 15, 1791, and form what is known as the "Bill of Rights."

Amendment I

Congress shall make no law respecting an establishment of religion, or prohibiting the free exercise thereof; or abridging the freedom of speech, or of the press; or the right of the people peaceably to assemble, and to petition the Government for a redress of grievances.

Amendment II

A well regulated Militia, being necessary to the security of a free State, the right of the people to keep and bear Arms, shall not be infringed.

Amendment III

No Soldier shall, in time of peace be quartered in any house, without the consent of the Owner, nor in time of war, but in a manner to be prescribed by law.

Amendment IV

The right of the people to be secure in their persons, houses, papers, and effects, against unreasonable searches and seizures, shall not be violated, and no Warrants shall issue, but upon probable cause, supported by Oath or affirmation, and particularly describing the place to be searched, and the persons or things to be seized.

Amendment V

No person shall be held to answer for a capital, or otherwise infamous crime, unless on a presentment or indictment of a Grand Jury, except in cases arising in the land or naval forces, or in the Militia, when in actual service in time of War or public danger; nor shall any person be subject for the same offence to be twice put in jeopardy of life or limb; nor shall be compelled in any criminal case to be a witness against himself, nor be deprived of life, liberty, or property, without due process of law; nor shall private property be taken for public use, without just compensation.

Amendment VI

In all criminal prosecutions, the accused shall enjoy the right to a speedy and public trial, by an impartial jury of the State and district wherein the crime shall have been committed, which district shall have been previously ascertained by law, and to be informed of the nature and cause of the accusation; to be confronted with the witnesses against him; to have compulsory process for obtaining witnesses in his favor, and to have the Assistance of Counsel for his defence.

Amendment VII

In Suits at common law, where the value in controversy shall exceed twenty dollars, the right of trial by jury shall be preserved, and no fact tried by a jury, shall be otherwise re-examined in any Court of the United States, than according to the rules of the common law.

Amendment VIII

Excessive bail shall not be required, nor excessive fines imposed, nor cruel and unusual punishments inflicted.

Amendment IX

The enumeration in the Constitution, of certain rights, shall not be construed to deny or disparage others retained by the people.

Amendment X

The powers not delegated to the United States by the Constitution, nor prohibited by it to the States, are reserved to the States respectively, or to the people.

Amendment XI

Passed by Congress March 4, 1794. Ratified February 7, 1795.

Note: Article III, section 2, of the Constitution was modified by amendment 11.

The Judicial power of the United States shall not be construed to extend to any suit in law or equity, commenced or prosecuted against one of the United States by Citizens of another State, or by Citizens or Subjects of any Foreign State.

Amendment XII

Passed by Congress December 9, 1803. Ratified June 15, 1804.

Note: A portion of Article II, section 1 of the Constitution was superseded by the 12th amendment.

The Electors shall meet in their respective states and vote by ballot for President and Vice-President, one of whom, at least, shall not be an inhabitant of the same state with themselves; they shall name in their ballots the person voted for as President, and in distinct ballots the person voted for as Vice-President, and they shall make distinct lists of all persons voted for as President, and of all persons voted for as Vice-President, and of the number of votes for each, which lists they shall sign and certify, and transmit sealed to the seat of the government of the United States, directed to the President of the Senate;—the President of the Senate shall, in the presence of the Senate and House of Representatives, open all the certificates and the votes shall then be counted;—The person having the greatest number of votes for President, shall be the President, if such number be a majority of the whole number of Electors appointed; and if no person have such majority, then from the persons having the highest numbers not exceeding three on the list of those voted for as President, the House of Representatives shall choose immediately, by ballot, the President. But in choosing the President, the votes shall be taken by states, the representation from each state having one vote; a quorum for this purpose shall consist of a member or members from two-thirds of the states, and a majority of all the states shall be necessary to a choice. [And if the House of Representatives shall not choose a President whenever the right of choice shall devolve upon them, before the fourth day of March next following, then the Vice-President shall act as President, as in case of the death or other constitutional disability of the President.—]* The person having the greatest number of votes as Vice-President, shall be the Vice-President, if such number be a majority of the whole number of Electors appointed, and if no person have a majority, then from the two highest numbers on the list, the Senate shall choose the Vice-President; a quorum for the purpose shall consist of two-thirds of the whole number of Senators, and a majority of the whole number shall be necessary to a choice. But no person constitutionally ineligible to the office of President shall be eligible to that of Vice-President of the United States.

*Superseded by section 3 of the 20th amendment.

Amendment XIII

Passed by Congress January 31, 1865. Ratified December 6, 1865.

Note: A portion of Article IV, section 2, of the Constitution was superseded by the 13th amendment.

Section 1.

Neither slavery nor involuntary servitude, except as a punishment for crime whereof the party shall have been duly convicted, shall exist within the United States, or any place subject to their jurisdiction.

Section 2.

Congress shall have power to enforce this article by appropriate legislation.

Amendment XIV

Passed by Congress June 13, 1866. Ratified July 9, 1868.

Note: Article I, section 2, of the Constitution was modified by section 2 of the 14th amendment.

Section 1.

All persons born or naturalized in the United States, and subject to the jurisdiction thereof, are citizens of the United States and of the State wherein they reside. No State shall make or enforce any law which shall abridge the privileges or immunities of citizens of the United States; nor shall any State deprive any person of life, liberty, or property, without due process of law; nor deny to any person within its jurisdiction the equal protection of the laws.

Section 2.

Representatives shall be apportioned among the several States according to their respective numbers, counting the whole number of persons in each State, excluding Indians not taxed. But when the right to vote at any election for the choice of electors for President and Vice-President of the United States, Representatives in Congress, the

Executive and Judicial officers of a State, or the members of the Legislature thereof, is denied to any of the male inhabitants of such State, being twenty-one years of age,* and citizens of the United States, or in any way abridged, except for participation in rebellion, or other crime, the basis of representation therein shall be reduced in the proportion which the number of such male citizens shall bear to the whole number of male citizens twenty-one years of age in such State.

Section 3.

No person shall be a Senator or Representative in Congress, or elector of President and Vice-President, or hold any office, civil or military, under the United States, or under any State, who, having previously taken an oath, as a member of Congress, or as an officer of the United States, or as a member of any State legislature, or as an executive or judicial officer of any State, to support the Constitution of the United States, shall have engaged in insurrection or rebellion against the same, or given aid or comfort to the enemies thereof. But Congress may by a vote of two-thirds of each House, remove such disability.

Section 4.

The validity of the public debt of the United States, authorized by law, including debts incurred for payment of pensions and bounties for services in suppressing insurrection or rebellion, shall not be questioned. But neither the United States nor any State shall assume or pay any debt or obligation incurred in aid of insurrection or rebellion against the United States, or any claim for the loss or emancipation of any slave; but all such debts, obligations and claims shall be held illegal and void.

Section 5.

The Congress shall have the power to enforce, by appropriate legislation, the provisions of this article.

*Changed by section 1 of the 26th amendment.

Amendment XV

Passed by Congress February 26, 1869. Ratified February 3, 1870.

Section 1.

The right of citizens of the United States to vote shall not be denied or abridged by the United States or by any State on account of race, color, or previous condition of servitude—

Section 2.

The Congress shall have the power to enforce this article by appropriate legislation.

Amendment XVI

Passed by Congress July 2, 1909. Ratified February 3, 1913.

Note: Article I, section 9, of the Constitution was modified by amendment 16.

The Congress shall have power to lay and collect taxes on incomes, from whatever source derived, without apportionment among the several States, and without regard to any census or enumeration.

Amendment XVII

Passed by Congress May 13, 1912. Ratified April 8, 1913.

Note: Article I, section 3, of the Constitution was modified by the 17th amendment.

The Senate of the United States shall be composed of two Senators from each State, elected by the people thereof, for six years; and each Senator shall have one vote. The electors in each State shall have the qualifications requisite for electors of the most numerous branch of the State legislatures.

When vacancies happen in the representation of any State in the Senate, the executive authority of such State shall issue writs of election to fill such vacancies: Provided, That the legislature of any State may empower the executive thereof to make temporary appointments until the people fill the vacancies by election as the legislature may direct.

This amendment shall not be so construed as to affect the election or term of any Senator chosen before it becomes valid as part of the Constitution.

Amendment XVIII

Passed by Congress December 18, 1917. Ratified January 16, 1919. Repealed by amendment 21.

Section 1.

After one year from the ratification of this article the manufacture, sale, or transportation of intoxicating liquors within, the importation thereof into, or the exportation thereof from the United States and all territory subject to the jurisdiction thereof for beverage purposes is hereby prohibited.

Section 2.

The Congress and the several States shall have concurrent power to enforce this article by appropriate legislation.

Section 3.

This article shall be inoperative unless it shall have been ratified as an amendment to the Constitution by the legislatures of the several States, as provided in the Constitution, within seven years from the date of the submission hereof to the States by the Congress.

Amendment XIX

Passed by Congress June 4, 1919. Ratified August 18, 1920.

The right of citizens of the United States to vote shall not be denied or abridged by the United States or by any State on account of sex.

Congress shall have power to enforce this article by appropriate legislation.

Amendment XX

Passed by Congress March 2, 1932. Ratified January 23, 1933.

Note: Article I, section 4, of the Constitution was modified by section 2 of this amendment. In addition, a portion of the 12th amendment was superseded by section 3.

Section 1.

The terms of the President and the Vice President shall end at noon on the 20th day of January, and the terms of Senators and Representatives at noon on the 3rd day of January, of the years in which such terms would have ended if this article had not been ratified; and the terms of their successors shall then begin.

Section 2.

The Congress shall assemble at least once in every year, and such meeting shall begin at noon on the 3d day of January, unless they shall by law appoint a different day.

Section 3.

If, at the time fixed for the beginning of the term of the President, the President elect shall have died, the Vice President elect shall become President. If a President shall not have been chosen before the time fixed for the beginning of his term, or if the President elect shall have failed to qualify, then the Vice President elect shall act as President until a President shall have qualified; and the Congress may by law provide for the case wherein neither a President elect nor a Vice President shall have qualified, declaring who shall then act as President, or the manner in which one who is to act shall be selected, and such person shall act accordingly until a President or Vice President shall have qualified.

Section 4.

The Congress may by law provide for the case of the death of any of the persons from whom the House of Representatives may choose a President whenever the right of choice shall have devolved upon them, and for the case of the death of any of the persons from whom the Senate may choose a Vice President whenever the right of choice shall have devolved upon them.

Section 5.

Sections 1 and 2 shall take effect on the 15th day of October following the ratification of this article.

Section 6.

This article shall be inoperative unless it shall have been ratified as an amendment to the Constitution by the legislatures of three-fourths of the several States within seven years from the date of its submission.

Amendment XXI

Passed by Congress February 20, 1933. Ratified December 5, 1933.

Section 1.

The eighteenth article of amendment to the Constitution of the United States is hereby repealed.

Section 2.

The transportation or importation into any State, Territory, or Possession of the United States for delivery or use therein of intoxicating liquors, in violation of the laws thereof, is hereby prohibited.

Section 3.

This article shall be inoperative unless it shall have been ratified as an amendment to the Constitution by conventions in the several States, as provided in the Constitution, within seven years from the date of the submission hereof to the States by the Congress.

Amendment XXII

Passed by Congress March 21, 1947. Ratified February 27, 1951.

Section 1.

No person shall be elected to the office of the President more than twice, and no person who has held the office of President, or acted as President, for more than two years of a term to which some other person was elected President shall be elected to the office of President more than once. But this Article shall not apply to any person holding the office of President when this Article was proposed by Congress, and shall not prevent any person who may be holding the office of President, or acting as President, during the term within which this Article becomes operative from holding the office of President or acting as President during the remainder of such term.

Section 2.

This article shall be inoperative unless it shall have been ratified as an amendment to the Constitution by the legislatures of three-fourths of the several States within seven years from the date of its submission to the States by the Congress.

Amendment XXIII

Passed by Congress June 16, 1960. Ratified March 29, 1961.

Section 1.

The District constituting the seat of Government of the United States shall appoint in such manner as Congress may direct:

A number of electors of President and Vice President equal to the whole number of Senators and Representatives in Congress to which the District would be entitled if it were a State, but in no event more than the least populous State; they shall be in addition to those appointed by the States, but they shall be considered, for the purposes of the election of President and Vice President, to be electors appointed by a State; and they shall meet in the District and perform such duties as provided by the twelfth article of amendment.

Section 2.

The Congress shall have power to enforce this article by appropriate legislation.

Amendment XXIV

Passed by Congress August 27, 1962. Ratified January 23, 1964.

Section 1.

The right of citizens of the United States to vote in any primary or other election for President or Vice President, for electors for President or Vice President, or for Senator or Representative in Congress, shall not be denied or abridged by the United States or any State by reason of failure to pay any poll tax or other tax.

Section 2.

The Congress shall have power to enforce this article by appropriate legislation.

Amendment XXV

Passed by Congress July 6, 1965. Ratified February 10, 1967.

Note: Article II, section 1, of the Constitution was affected by the 25th amendment.

Section 1.

In case of the removal of the President from office or of his death or resignation, the Vice President shall become President.

Section 2.

Whenever there is a vacancy in the office of the Vice President, the President shall nominate a Vice President who shall take office upon confirmation by a majority vote of both Houses of Congress.

Section 3.

Whenever the President transmits to the President pro tempore of the Senate and the Speaker of the House of Representatives his written declaration that he is unable to discharge the powers and duties of his office, and until he transmits to them a written declaration to the contrary, such powers and duties shall be discharged by the Vice President as Acting President.

Section 4.

Whenever the Vice President and a majority of either the principal officers of the executive departments or of such other body as Congress may by law provide, transmit to the President pro tempore of the Senate and the Speaker of the House of

Representatives their written declaration that the President is unable to discharge the powers and duties of his office, the Vice President shall immediately assume the powers and duties of the office as Acting President.

Thereafter, when the President transmits to the President pro tempore of the Senate and the Speaker of the House of Representatives his written declaration that no inability exists, he shall resume the powers and duties of his office unless the Vice President and a majority of either the principal officers of the executive department or of such other body as Congress may by law provide, transmit within four days to the President pro tempore of the Senate and the Speaker of the House of Representatives their written declaration that the President is unable to discharge the powers and duties of his office. Thereupon Congress shall decide the issue, assembling within forty-eight hours for that purpose if not in session. If the Congress, within twenty-one days after receipt of the latter written declaration, or, if Congress is not in session, within twenty-one days after Congress is required to assemble, determines by two-thirds vote of both Houses that the President is unable to discharge the powers and duties of his office, the Vice President shall continue to discharge the same as Acting President; otherwise, the President shall resume the powers and duties of his office.

Amendment XXVI

Passed by Congress March 23, 1971. Ratified July 1, 1971.

Note: Amendment 14, section 2, of the Constitution was modified by section 1 of the 26th amendment.

Section 1.

The right of citizens of the United States, who are eighteen years of age or older, to vote shall not be denied or abridged by the United States or by any State on account of age.

Section 2.

The Congress shall have power to enforce this article by appropriate legislation.

Amendment XXVII

Originally proposed Sept. 25, 1789. Ratified May 7, 1992.

No law, varying the compensation for the services of the Senators and Representatives, shall take effect, until an election of representatives shall have intervened.

Source: *Constitution of the United States,* The Charters of Freedom, http://www.archives.gov/exhibits/charters/constitution_transcript.html (last visited September 10, 2014).

APPENDIX C
GLOSSARY OF LEGAL TERMS IN PLAIN ENGLISH

A

Acquittal A jury verdict that a criminal defendant is not guilty, or the finding of a judge that the evidence is insufficient to support a conviction.

Active judge A judge in the full-time service of the court. Compare to senior judge.

Administrative Office of the United States Courts (AO) The federal agency responsible for collecting court statistics, administering the federal courts' budget, and performing many other administrative and programmatic functions, under the direction and supervision of the Judicial Conference of the United States.

Admissible A term used to describe evidence that may be considered by a jury or judge in civil and criminal cases.

Adversary proceeding A lawsuit arising in or related to a bankruptcy case that begins by filing a complaint with the court; that is, a "trial" that takes place within the context of a bankruptcy case.

Affidavit A written or printed statement made under oath.

Affirmed In the practice of the court of appeals, it means that the court of appeals has concluded that the lower court decision is correct and will stand as rendered by the lower court.

Alternate juror A juror selected in the same manner as a regular juror who hears all the evidence but does not help decide the case unless called on to replace a regular juror.

Alternative dispute resolution (ADR) A procedure for settling a dispute outside the courtroom. Most forms of ADR are not binding, and involve referral of the case to a neutral party such as an arbitrator or mediator.

Amicus curiae Latin for "friend of the court." It is advice formally offered to the court in a brief filed by an entity interested in, but not a party to, the case.

Answer The formal written statement by a defendant in a civil case that responds to a complaint, articulating the grounds for defense.

Appeal A request made after a trial by a party that has lost on one or more issues that a higher court review the decision to determine if it was correct. To make such a request is "to appeal" or "to take an appeal." One who appeals is called the "appellant"; the other party is the "appellee."

Appellant The party who appeals a district court's decision, usually seeking reversal of that decision.

Appellate About appeals; an appellate court has the power to review the judgment of a lower court (trial court) or tribunal. For example, the U.S. circuit courts of appeals review the decisions of the U.S. district courts.

Appellee The party who opposes an appellant's appeal, and who seeks to persuade the appeals court to affirm the district court's decision.

Arraignment A proceeding in which a criminal defendant is brought into court, told of the charges in an indictment or information, and asked to plead guilty or not guilty.

Article III judge A federal judge who is appointed for life, during "good behavior," under Article III of the Constitution. Article III judges are nominated by the President and confirmed by the Senate.

Assets Property of all kinds, including real and personal, tangible and intangible.

Assume An agreement to continue performing duties under a contract or lease.

Automatic stay An injunction that automatically stops lawsuits, foreclosures, garnishments, and most collection activities against the debtor the moment a bankruptcy petition is filed.

B

Bail The release, prior to trial, of a person accused of a crime, under specified conditions designed to assure that person's appearance in court when required. Also can refer to the amount of bond money posted as a financial condition of pretrial release.

Bankruptcy A legal procedure for dealing with debt problems of individuals and businesses; specifically, a case filed under one of the chapters of Title 11 of the United States Code (the Bankruptcy Code).

Bankruptcy administrator An officer of the Judiciary serving in the judicial districts of Alabama and North Carolina who, like the United States trustee, is responsible for supervising the administration of bankruptcy cases, estates, and trustees; monitoring plans and disclosure statements; monitoring creditors' committees; monitoring fee applications; and performing other statutory duties.

Bankruptcy code The informal name for Title 11 of the United States Code (11 U.S.C. §§ 101-1330), the federal bankruptcy law.

Bankruptcy court The bankruptcy judges in regular active service in each district; a unit of the district court.

Bankruptcy estate All interests of the debtor in property at the time of the bankruptcy filing. The estate technically becomes the temporary legal owner of all of the debtor's property.

Bankruptcy judge A judicial officer of the United States district court who is the court official with decision-making power over federal bankruptcy cases.

Bankruptcy petition A formal request for the protection of the federal bankruptcy laws. (There is an official form for bankruptcy petitions.)

Bankruptcy trustee A private individual or corporation appointed in all Chapter 7 and Chapter 13 cases to represent the interests of the bankruptcy estate and the debtor's creditors.

Bench trial A trial without a jury, in which the judge serves as the fact-finder.

Brief A written statement submitted in a trial or appellate proceeding that explains one side's legal and factual arguments.

Burden of proof The duty to prove disputed facts. In civil cases, a plaintiff generally has the burden of proving his or her case. In criminal cases, the government has the burden of proving the defendant's guilt. (See standard of proof.)

Business bankruptcy A bankruptcy case in which the debtor is a business or an individual involved in business and the debts are for business purposes.

C

Capital offense A crime punishable by death.

Case file A complete collection of every document filed in court in a case.

Case law The law as established in previous court decisions. A synonym for legal precedent. Akin to common law, which springs from tradition and judicial decisions.

Caseload The number of cases handled by a judge or a court.

Cause of action A legal claim.

Chambers The offices of a judge and his or her staff.

Chapter 7 The chapter of the Bankruptcy Code providing for "liquidation," that is, the sale of a debtor's nonexempt property and the distribution of the proceeds to creditors. In order to be eligible for Chapter 7, the debtor must satisfy a "means test." The court will evaluate the debtor's income and expenses to determine if the debtor may proceed under Chapter 7.

Chapter 7 trustee A person appointed in a Chapter 7 case to represent the interests of the bankruptcy estate and the creditors. The trustee's responsibilities include reviewing the debtor's petition and schedules, liquidating the property of the estate, and making distributions to creditors. The trustee may also bring actions against creditors or the debtor to recover property of the bankruptcy estate.

Chapter 9 The chapter of the Bankruptcy Code providing for reorganization of municipalities (which includes cities and towns, as well as villages, counties, taxing districts, municipal utilities, and school districts).

Chapter 11 A reorganization bankruptcy, usually involving a corporation or partnership. A Chapter 11 debtor usually proposes a plan of reorganization to keep its business alive and pay creditors over time. Individuals or people in business can also seek relief in Chapter 11.

Chapter 12 The chapter of the Bankruptcy Code providing for adjustment of debts of a "family farmer" or "family fisherman," as the terms are defined in the Bankruptcy Code.

Chapter 13 The chapter of the Bankruptcy Code providing for the adjustment of debts of an individual with regular income, often referred to as a "wage-earner" plan. Chapter 13 allows a debtor to keep property and use his or her disposable income to pay debts over time, usually three to five years.

Chapter 13 trustee A person appointed to administer a Chapter 13 case. A Chapter 13 trustee's responsibilities are similar to those of a Chapter 7 trustee; however, a Chapter 13 trustee has the additional responsibilities of overseeing the debtor's plan, receiving payments from debtors, and disbursing plan payments to creditors.

Chapter 15 The chapter of the Bankruptcy Code dealing with cases of cross-border insolvency.

Chief judge The judge who has primary responsibility for the administration of a court; chief judges are determined by seniority.

Claim A creditor's assertion of a right to payment from a debtor or the debtor's property.

Class action A lawsuit in which one or more members of a large group, or class, of individuals or other entities sue on behalf of the entire class. The district court must find that the claims of the class members contain questions of law or fact in common before the lawsuit can proceed as a class action.

Clerk of court The court officer who oversees administrative functions, especially managing the flow of cases through the court. The clerk's office is often called a court's central nervous system.

Collateral Property that is promised as security for the satisfaction of a debt.

Common law The legal system that originated in England and is now in use in the United States, which relies on the articulation of legal principles in a historical succession of judicial decisions. Common law principles can be changed by legislation.

Community service A special condition the court imposes that requires an individual to work—without pay—for a civic or nonprofit organization.

Complaint A written statement that begins a civil lawsuit, in which the plaintiff details the claims against the defendant.

Concurrent sentence Prison terms for two or more offenses to be served at the same time, rather than one after the other. Example: Two five-year sentences and one three-year sentence, if served concurrently, result in a maximum of five years behind bars.

Confirmation Approval of a plan of reorganization by a bankruptcy judge.

Consecutive sentence Prison terms for two or more offenses to be served one after the other. Example: Two five-year sentences and one three-year sentence, if served consecutively, result in a maximum of 13 years behind bars.

Consumer bankruptcy A bankruptcy case filed to reduce or eliminate debts that are primarily consumer debts.

Consumer debts Debts incurred for personal, as opposed to business, needs.

Contingent claim A claim that may be owed by the debtor under certain circumstances (e.g., where the debtor is a cosigner on another person's loan and that person fails to pay).

Contract An agreement between two or more people that creates an obligation to do or not to do a particular thing.

Conviction A judgment of guilt against a criminal defendant.

Counsel Legal advice; a term also used to refer to the lawyers in a case.

Court Government entity authorized to resolve legal disputes. Judges sometimes use "court" to refer to themselves in the third person, as in "the court has read the briefs."

Court reporter A person who makes a word-for-word record of what is said in court, generally by using a stenographic machine, shorthand, or audio recording, and then produces a transcript of the proceedings upon request.

Count An allegation in an indictment or information, charging a defendant with a crime. An indictment or information may contain allegations that the defendant committed more than one crime. Each allegation is referred to as a count.

Creditor A person to whom or business to which the debtor owes money or that claims to be owed money by the debtor.

Credit counseling Generally refers to two events in individual bankruptcy cases: (1) the "individual or group briefing" from a nonprofit budget and credit counseling agency that individual debtors must attend prior to filing under any chapter of the Bankruptcy Code; and (2) the "instructional course in personal financial management" in Chapters 7 and 13 that an individual debtor must complete before a discharge is entered. There are exceptions to both requirements for certain categories of debtors, exigent circumstances, or if the U.S. trustee or bankruptcy administrator have determined that there are insufficient approved credit counseling agencies available to provide the necessary counseling.

D

Damages Money that a defendant pays a plaintiff in a civil case if the plaintiff has won. Damages may be compensatory (for loss or injury) or punitive (to punish and deter future misconduct).

Debtor A person who has filed a petition for relief under the Bankruptcy Code.

Defendant An individual (or business) against whom a lawsuit is filed.

Debtor's plan A debtor's detailed description of how the debtor proposes to pay creditors' claims over a fixed period of time.

Declaratory judgment A judge's statement about someone's rights. For example, a plaintiff may seek a declaratory judgment that a particular statute, as written, violates some constitutional right.

De facto Latin, meaning "in fact" or "actually." Something that exists in fact but not as a matter of law.

Default judgment A judgment awarding a plaintiff the relief sought in the complaint because the defendant has failed to appear in court or otherwise respond to the complaint.

Defendant In a civil case, the person or organization against whom the plaintiff brings suit; in a criminal case, the person accused of the crime.

De jure Latin, meaning "in law." Something that exists by operation of law.

De novo Latin, meaning "anew." A trial de novo is a completely new trial. Appellate review de novo implies no deference to the trial judge's ruling.

Deposition An oral statement made before an officer who is authorized by law to administer oaths. Such statements are often taken to examine potential witnesses, to obtain discovery, or to be used later in trial. See discovery.

Discharge A release of a debtor from personal liability for certain dischargeable debts. Notable exceptions to dischargeability are taxes and student loans. A discharge releases a debtor from personal liability for certain debts known as dischargeable debts and prevents the creditors owed those debts from taking any action against the debtor or the debtor's property to collect the debts. The discharge also prohibits creditors from communicating with the debtor regarding the debt, including through telephone calls, letters, and personal contact.

Dischargeable debt A debt for which the Bankruptcy Code allows the debtor's personal liability to be eliminated.

Disclosure statement A written document prepared by the Chapter 11 debtor or other plan proponent that is designed to provide "adequate information" to creditors to enable them to evaluate the Chapter 11 plan of reorganization.

Discovery Procedures used to obtain disclosure of evidence before trial.

Dismissal with prejudice Court action that prevents an identical lawsuit from being filed later.

Dismissal without prejudice Court action that allows the later filing.

Disposable income Income not reasonably necessary for the maintenance or support of the debtor or dependents. If the debtor operates a business, disposable income is defined as those amounts over and above what is necessary for the payment of ordinary operating expenses.

Docket A log containing the complete history of each case in the form of brief chronological entries summarizing the court proceedings.

Due process In criminal law, the constitutional guarantee that a defendant will receive a fair and impartial trial. In civil law, the legal rights of someone who confronts an adverse action threatening liberty or property.

E

En banc French, meaning "on the bench." All judges of an appellate court sitting together to hear a case, as opposed to the routine disposition by panels of three judges. In the Ninth Circuit, an en banc panel consists of 11 randomly selected judges.

Equitable Pertaining to civil suits in "equity" rather than in "law." In English legal history, the courts of "law" could order the payment of damages and could afford no other remedy (see damages). A separate court of "equity" could order someone to do something or to cease to do something (e.g., injunction). In American jurisprudence, the federal courts have both legal and equitable power, but the distinction is still an important one. For example, a trial by jury is normally available in "law" cases but not in "equity" cases.

Equity The value of a debtor's interest in property that remains after liens and other creditors' interests are considered. (Example: If a house valued at $60,000 is subject to a $30,000 mortgage, there is $30,000 of equity.)

Evidence Information presented in testimony or in documents that is used to persuade the fact finder (judge or jury) to decide the case in favor of one side or the other.

Exclusionary rule Doctrine that says evidence obtained in violation of a criminal defendant's constitutional or statutory rights is not admissible at trial.

Exculpatory evidence Evidence indicating that a defendant did not commit the crime.

Executory contracts Contracts or leases under which both parties to the agreement have duties remaining to be performed. If a contract or lease is executory, a debtor may assume it (keep the contract) or reject it (terminate the contract).

Exempt assets Property that a debtor is allowed to retain, free from the claims of creditors who do not have liens on the property.

Exemptions, exempt property Certain property owned by an individual debtor that the Bankruptcy Code or applicable state law permits the debtor to keep from unsecured creditors. For example, in some states the debtor may be able to exempt all or a portion of the equity in the debtor's primary residence (homestead exemption), or some or all "tools of the trade" used by the debtor to make a living (i.e., auto tools for an auto mechanic or dental tools for a dentist). The availability and amount of property the debtor may exempt depends on the state the debtor lives in.

Ex parte A proceeding brought before a court by one party only, without notice to or challenge by the other side.

F

Face sheet filing A bankruptcy case filed either without schedules or with incomplete schedules listing few creditors and debts. (Face sheet filings are often made to delay an eviction or foreclosure.)

Family farmer An individual, individual and spouse, corporation, or partnership engaged in a farming operation that meets certain debt limits and other statutory criteria for filing a petition under Chapter 12.

Federal public defender An attorney employed by the federal courts on a full-time basis to provide legal defense to defendants who are unable to afford counsel. The judiciary administers the federal defender program pursuant to the Criminal Justice Act.

Federal public defender organization As provided for in the Criminal Justice Act, an organization established within a federal judicial circuit to represent criminal defendants who cannot afford an adequate defense. Each organization is supervised by a federal public defender appointed by the court of appeals for the circuit.

Federal question jurisdiction Jurisdiction given to federal courts in cases involving the interpretation and application of the U.S. Constitution, acts of Congress, and treaties.

Felony A serious crime, usually punishable by at least one year in prison.

File To place a paper in the official custody of the clerk of court to enter into the files or records of a case.

Fraudulent transfer A transfer of a debtor's property made with intent to defraud or for which the debtor receives less than the transferred property's value.

Fresh start The characterization of a debtor's status after bankruptcy (i.e., free of most debts). Giving debtors a fresh start is one purpose of the Bankruptcy Code.

G

Grand jury A body of 16 to 23 citizens who listen to evidence of criminal allegations, which is presented by the prosecutors, and determine whether there is probable cause to believe an individual committed an offense. See also indictment and U.S. attorney.

H

Habeas corpus Latin, meaning "you have the body." A writ of habeas corpus generally is a judicial order forcing law enforcement authorities to produce a prisoner they are holding, and to justify the prisoner's continued confinement. Federal judges receive petitions for a writ of habeas corpus from state prison inmates who say their state prosecutions violated federally protected rights in some way.

Hearsay Evidence presented by a witness who did not see or hear the incident in question but heard about it from someone else. With some exceptions, hearsay generally is not admissible as evidence at trial.

Home confinement A special condition the court imposes that requires an individual to remain at home except for certain approved activities, such as work and medical appointments. Home confinement may include the use of electronic monitoring equipment—a transmitter attached to the wrist or the ankle—to help ensure that the person stays at home as required.

I

Impeachment 1. The process of calling a witness's testimony into doubt (e.g., if the attorney can show that the witness may have fabricated portions of his testimony, the witness is said to be "impeached"); 2. The constitutional process whereby the House of Representatives may "impeach" (accuse of misconduct) high officers of the federal government, who are then tried by the Senate.

In camera Latin, meaning "in a judge's chambers." Often means outside the presence of a jury and the public; in private.

Inculpatory evidence Evidence indicating that a defendant did commit the crime.

Indictment The formal charge issued by a grand jury stating that there is enough evidence that the defendant committed the crime to justify having a trial; it is used primarily for felonies. See also information.

In forma pauperis Latin, meaning "in the manner of a pauper." Permission given by the court to a person to file a case without payment of the required court fees because the person cannot pay them.

Information A formal accusation by a government attorney that the defendant committed a misdemeanor. See also indictment.

Injunction A court order preventing one or more named parties from taking some action. A preliminary injunction often is issued to allow fact-finding, so a judge can determine whether a permanent injunction is justified.

Insider (of corporate debtor) A director, officer, or person in control of the debtor; a partnership in which the debtor is a general partner; a general partner of the debtor; or a relative of a general partner, director, officer, or person in control of the debtor.

Insider (of individual debtor) Any relative of the debtor or of a general partner of the debtor; partnership in which the debtor is a general partner; general partner of the debtor; or corporation of which the debtor is a director, officer, or person in control.

Interrogatories A form of discovery consisting of written questions to be answered in writing and under oath.

Issue 1. The disputed point between parties in a lawsuit; 2. To send out officially, as in a court issuing an order.

J

Joint administration A court-approved mechanism under which two or more cases can be administered together. (Assuming no conflicts of interest, these separate businesses or individuals can pool their resources, hire the same professionals, etc.)

Joint petition One bankruptcy petition filed by a husband and wife together.

Judge An official of the Judicial branch with the authority to decide lawsuits brought before courts. Used generically, the term judge may also refer to all judicial officers, including Supreme Court justices.

Judgeship The position of judge. By statute, Congress authorizes the number of judgeships for each district and appellate court.

Judgment The official decision of a court finally resolving the dispute between the parties to the lawsuit.

Judicial Conference of the United States The policy-making entity for the federal court system. A 27-judge body whose presiding officer is the Chief Justice of the United States.

Jurisdiction The legal authority of a court to hear and decide a certain type of case. It also is used as a synonym for venue, meaning the geographic area over which the court has territorial jurisdiction to decide cases.

Jurisprudence The study of law and the structure of the legal system.

Jury The group of persons selected to hear the evidence in a trial and render a verdict on matters of fact. See also grand jury.

Jury instructions A judge's directions to the jury before it begins deliberations regarding the factual questions it must answer and the legal rules that it must apply.

L

Lawsuit A legal action started by a plaintiff against a defendant based on a complaint that the defendant failed to perform a legal duty, which resulted in harm to the plaintiff.

Lien A charge on specific property that is designed to secure payment of a debt or performance of an obligation. A debtor may still be responsible for a lien after a discharge.

Litigation A case, controversy, or lawsuit. Participants (plaintiffs and defendants) in lawsuits are called litigants.

Liquidation The sale of a debtor's property with the proceeds to be used for the benefit of creditors.

Liquidated claim A creditor's claim for a fixed amount of money.

M

Magistrate judge A judicial officer of a district court who conducts initial proceedings in criminal cases, decides criminal misdemeanor cases, conducts many pretrial civil and criminal matters on behalf of district judges, and decides civil cases with the consent of the parties.

Means test Section 707(b)(2) of the Bankruptcy Code applies a "means test" to determine whether an individual debtor's Chapter 7 filing is presumed to be an abuse of the Bankruptcy Code requiring dismissal or conversion of the case (generally to Chapter 13). Abuse is presumed if the debtor's aggregate current monthly income (see definition above) over 5 years, net of certain statutorily allowed expenses is more than (i) $10,000, or (ii) 25 percent of the debtor's nonpriority unsecured debt, as long as that amount is at least $6,000. The debtor may rebut a presumption of abuse only by a showing of special circumstances that justify additional expenses or adjustments of current monthly income.

Mental health treatment Special condition the court imposes to require an individual to undergo evaluation and treatment for a mental disorder. Treatment may include psychiatric, psychological, and sex offense–specific evaluations, inpatient or outpatient counseling, and medication.

Misdemeanor An offense punishable by one year of imprisonment or less. See also felony.

Mistrial An invalid trial, caused by fundamental error. When a mistrial is declared, the trial must start again with the selection of a new jury.

Moot Not subject to a court ruling because the controversy has not actually arisen, or has ended.

Motion A request by a litigant to a judge for a decision on an issue relating to the case.

Motion to lift the automatic stay A request by a creditor to allow the creditor to take action against the debtor or the debtor's property that would otherwise be prohibited by the automatic stay.

Motion in limine A pretrial motion requesting the court to prohibit the other side from presenting, or even referring to, evidence on matters said to be so highly prejudicial that no steps taken by the judge can prevent the jury from being unduly influenced.

N

No-asset case A Chapter 7 case in which there are no assets available to satisfy any portion of the creditors' unsecured claims.

Nolo contendere Latin, meaning "no contest." A plea of nolo contendere has the same effect as a plea of guilty, as far as the criminal sentence is concerned, but may not be considered as an admission of guilt for any other purpose.

Nondischargeable debt A debt that cannot be eliminated in bankruptcy. Examples include a home mortgage, debts for alimony or child support, certain taxes, debts for most government-funded or guaranteed educational loans or benefit overpayments, debts arising from death or personal injury caused by driving while intoxicated or under the influence of drugs, and debts for restitution or a criminal fine included in a sentence on the debtor's conviction of a crime. Some debts, such as debts for money or property obtained by false pretenses and debts for fraud or defalcation while acting in a fiduciary capacity, may be declared nondischargeable only if a creditor timely files and prevails in a nondischargeability action.

Nonexempt assets Property of a debtor that can be liquidated to satisfy claims of creditors.

O

Objection to dischargeability A trustee's or creditor's objection to the debtor being released from personal liability for certain dischargeable debts. Common reasons include allegations that the debt to be discharged was incurred by false pretenses or that debt arose because of the debtor's fraud while acting as a fiduciary.

Objection to exemptions A trustee's or creditor's objection to the debtor's attempt to claim certain property as exempt from liquidation by the trustee to creditors.

Opinion A judge's written explanation of the decision of the court. Because a case may be heard by three or more judges in the court of appeals, the opinion in appellate decisions can take several forms. If all the judges completely agree on the result, one judge will write the opinion for all. If all the judges do not agree, the formal decision will be based upon the view of the majority, and one member of the majority will write the opinion. The judges who did not agree with the majority may write separately in dissenting or concurring opinions to present their views. A dissenting opinion disagrees with the majority opinion because of the reasoning and/or the principles of law the majority used to decide the case. A concurring opinion agrees with the decision of the majority opinion, but offers further comment or clarification or even an entirely different reason for reaching the same result. Only the majority opinion can serve as binding precedent in future cases. See also precedent.

Oral argument An opportunity for lawyers to summarize their position before the court and also to answer the judges' questions.

P

Panel 1. In appellate cases, a group of judges (usually three) assigned to decide the case; 2. In the jury selection process, the group of potential jurors; 3. The list of attorneys who are both available and qualified to serve as court-appointed counsel for criminal defendants who cannot afford their own counsel.

Parole The release of a prison inmate—granted by the U.S. Parole Commission—after the inmate has completed part of his or her sentence in a federal prison. When the parolee is released to the community, he or she is placed under the supervision of a U.S. probation officer.

The Sentencing Reform Act of 1984 abolished parole in favor of a determinate sentencing system in which the sentence is set by sentencing guidelines. Now, without the option of parole, the term of imprisonment the court imposes is the actual time the person spends in prison.

Party in interest A party who has standing to be heard by the court in a matter to be decided in the bankruptcy case. The debtor, U.S. trustee or bankruptcy administrator, case trustee, and creditors are parties in interest for most matters.

Petition preparer A business not authorized to practice law that prepares bankruptcy petitions.

Per curiam Latin, meaning "for the court." In appellate courts, often refers to an unsigned opinion.

Peremptory challenge A district court may grant each side in a civil or criminal trial the right to exclude a certain number of prospective jurors without cause or giving a reason.

Petit jury (or trial jury) A group of citizens who hear the evidence presented by both sides at trial and determine the facts in dispute. Federal criminal juries consist of 12 persons. Federal civil juries consist of at least six persons.

Petition The document that initiates the filing of a bankruptcy proceeding, setting forth basic information regarding the debtor, including name, address, chapter under which the case is filed, and estimated amount of assets and liabilities.

Petty offense A federal misdemeanor punishable by six months or less in prison.

Plaintiff A person or business that files a formal complaint with the court.

Plan A debtor's detailed description of how the debtor proposes to pay creditors' claims over a fixed period of time.

Plea In a criminal case, the defendant's statement pleading "guilty" or "not guilty" in answer to the charges. See also nolo contendere.

Pleadings Written statements filed with the court that describe a party's legal or factual assertions about the case.

Postpetition transfer A transfer of the debtor's property made after the commencement of the case.

Prebankruptcy planning The arrangement (or rearrangement) of a debtor's property to allow the debtor to take maximum advantage of exemptions. (Prebankruptcy planning typically includes converting nonexempt assets into exempt assets.)

Precedent A court decision in an earlier case with facts and legal issues similar to a dispute currently before a court. Judges will generally "follow precedent," meaning that they use the principles established in earlier cases to decide new cases that have similar facts and raise similar legal issues. A judge will disregard precedent if a party can show that the earlier case was wrongly decided, or that it differed in some significant way from the current case.

Preferential debt payment A debt payment made to a creditor in the 90-day period before a debtor files bankruptcy (or within one year if the creditor was an insider) that gives the creditor more than the creditor would receive in the debtor's Chapter 7 case.

Presentence report A report prepared by a court's probation officer, after a person has been convicted of an offense, summarizing for the court the background information needed to determine the appropriate sentence.

Pretrial conference A meeting of the judge and lawyers to plan the trial, to discuss which matters should be presented to the jury, to review proposed evidence and witnesses, and to set a trial schedule. Typically, the judge and the parties also discuss the possibility of settlement of the case.

Pretrial services A function of the federal courts that takes place at the very start of the criminal justice process—after a person has been arrested and charged with a federal crime and before he or she goes to trial. Pretrial services officers focus on investigating the backgrounds of these persons to help the court determine whether to release or detain them while they await trial. The decision is based on whether these individuals are likely to flee or pose a threat to the community. If the court orders release, a pretrial services officer supervises the person in the community until he or she returns to court.

Priority The Bankruptcy Code's statutory ranking of unsecured claims that determines the order in which unsecured claims will be paid if there is not enough money to pay all unsecured claims in full.

Priority claim An unsecured claim that is entitled to be paid ahead of other unsecured claims that are not entitled to priority status. Priority refers to the order in which these unsecured claims are to be paid.

Probation Sentencing option in the federal courts. With probation, instead of sending an individual to prison, the court releases the person to the community and orders him or her to complete a period of supervision monitored by a U.S. probation officer and to abide by certain conditions.

Probation officer Officers of the probation office of a court. Probation officer duties include conducting presentence investigations, preparing presentence reports on convicted defendants, and supervising released defendants.

Procedure The rules for conducting a lawsuit; there are rules of civil procedure, criminal procedure, evidence, bankruptcy, and appellate procedure.

Proof of claim A written statement describing the reason a debtor owes a creditor money, which typically sets forth the amount of money owed. (There is an official form for this purpose.)

Pro per A slang expression sometimes used to refer to a pro se litigant. It is a corruption of the Latin phrase "in propria persona."

Property of the estate All legal or equitable interests of the debtor in property as of the commencement of the case.

Pro se Representing oneself. Serving as one's own lawyer.

Prosecute To charge someone with a crime. A prosecutor tries a criminal case on behalf of the government.

Pro tem Temporary.

R

Reaffirmation agreement An agreement by a debtor to continue paying a dischargeable debt after the bankruptcy, usually to keep collateral or mortgaged property that would otherwise be subject to repossession.

Record A written account of the proceedings in a case, including all pleadings, evidence, and exhibits submitted in the course of the case.

Redemption A procedure in a Chapter 7 case whereby a debtor removes a secured creditor's lien on collateral by paying the creditor the value of the property. The debtor may then retain the property.

Remand Send back.

Reverse The act of a court setting aside the decision of a lower court. A reversal is often accompanied by a remand to the lower court for further proceedings.

S

Sanction A penalty or other type of enforcement used to bring about compliance with the law or with rules and regulations.

Schedules Lists submitted by the debtor along with the petition (or shortly thereafter), showing the debtor's assets, liabilities, and other financial information. (There are official forms a debtor must use.)

Secured creditor A secured creditor is an individual or business that holds a claim against the debtor that is secured by a lien on property of the estate. The property subject to the lien is the secured creditor's collateral.

Secured debt Debt backed by a mortgage, pledge of collateral, or other lien; debt for which the creditor has the right to pursue specific pledged property upon default. Examples include home mortgages, auto loans and tax liens.

Senior judge A federal judge who, after attaining the requisite age and length of judicial experience, takes senior status, thus creating a vacancy among a court's active judges. A senior judge retains the judicial office and may cut back his or her workload by as much as 75 percent, but many opt to keep a larger caseload.

Sentence The punishment ordered by a court for a defendant convicted of a crime.

Sentencing guidelines A set of rules and principles established by the United States Sentencing Commission that trial judges use to determine the sentence for a convicted defendant.

Service of process The delivery of writs or summonses to the appropriate party.

Settlement Parties to a lawsuit resolve their dispute without having a trial. Settlements often involve the payment of compensation by one party in at least partial satisfaction of the other party's claims, but usually do not include the admission of fault.

Sequester To separate. Sometimes juries are sequestered from outside influences during their deliberations.

Small business case A special type of Chapter 11 case in which there is no creditors' committee (or the creditors' committee is deemed inactive by the court) and in which the debtor is subject to more oversight by the U.S. trustee than other Chapter 11 debtors. The Bankruptcy Code contains certain provisions designed to reduce the time a small business debtor is in bankruptcy.

Statement of financial affairs A series of questions the debtor must answer in writing concerning sources of income, transfers of property, lawsuits by creditors, etc. (There is an official form a debtor must use.)

Statement of intention A declaration made by a Chapter 7 debtor concerning plans for dealing with consumer debts that are secured by property of the estate.

Standard of proof Degree of proof required. In criminal cases, prosecutors must prove a defendant's guilt "beyond a reasonable doubt." The majority of civil lawsuits require proof "by a preponderance of the evidence" (50 percent plus), but in some cases the standard is higher and requires "clear and convincing" proof.

Statute A law passed by a legislature.

Statute of limitations The time within which a lawsuit must be filed or a criminal prosecution begun. The deadline can vary, depending on the type of civil case or the crime charged.

Sua sponte Latin, meaning "of its own will." Often refers to a court taking an action in a case without being asked to do so by either side.

Subordination The act or process by which a person's rights or claims are ranked below those of others.

Subpoena A command, issued under a court's authority, to a witness to appear and give testimony.

Subpoena duces tecum A command to a witness to appear and produce documents.

Substance abuse treatment A special condition the court imposes that requires an individual to undergo testing and treatment for abuse of illegal drugs, prescription drugs, or alcohol. Treatment may include inpatient or outpatient counseling and detoxification.

Substantial abuse The characterization of a bankruptcy case filed by an individual whose debts are primarily consumer debts, where the court finds that the granting of relief would be an abuse of Chapter 7 because, for example, the debtor can pay its debts.

Substantive consolidation Putting the assets and liabilities of two or more related debtors into a single pool to pay creditors. (Courts are reluctant to allow substantive consolidation because the action must justify not only the benefit that one set of creditors receives but also the harm that other creditors suffer as a result.)

Summary judgment A decision made on the basis of statements and evidence presented for the record without a trial. It is used when it is not necessary to resolve any factual disputes in the case. Summary judgment is granted when—on the undisputed facts in the record—one party is entitled to judgment as a matter of law.

Supervised release Term of supervision served after a person is released from prison. The court imposes supervised release during sentencing in addition to the sentence of imprisonment. Unlike parole, supervised release does not replace a portion of the sentence of imprisonment but is in addition to the time spent in prison. U.S. probation officers supervise people on supervised release.

T

Temporary restraining order Akin to a preliminary injunction, it is a judge's short-term order forbidding certain actions until a full hearing can be conducted. Often referred to as a TRO.

Testimony Evidence presented orally by witnesses during trials or before grand juries.

Toll See statute of limitations.

Tort A civil, not criminal, wrong. A negligent or intentional injury against a person or property, with the exception of breach of contract.

Transfer Any mode or means by which a debtor disposes of or parts with his or her property.

Transcript A written, word-for-word record of what was said, either in a proceeding such as a trial or during some other formal conversation, such as a hearing or oral deposition.

Trustee The representative of the bankruptcy estate who exercises statutory powers, principally for the benefit of the unsecured creditors, under the general supervision of the court and the direct supervision of the U.S. trustee or bankruptcy administrator. The trustee is a private individual or corporation appointed in all Chapter 7, Chapter 12, and Chapter 13 cases and some Chapter 11 cases. The trustee's responsibilities include reviewing the debtor's petition and schedules and bringing actions against creditors or the debtor to recover property of the bankruptcy estate. In Chapter 7, the trustee liquidates property of the estate and makes distributions to creditors. Trustees in Chapter 12 and 13 have similar duties to a Chapter 7 trustee and the additional responsibilities of overseeing the debtor's plan, receiving payments from debtors, and disbursing plan payments to creditors.

Typing service A business not authorized to practice law that prepares bankruptcy petitions.

U

U.S. attorney A lawyer appointed by the President in each judicial district to prosecute and defend cases for the federal government. The U.S. Attorney employs a staff of Assistant U.S. Attorneys who appear as the government's attorneys in individual cases.

U.S. trustee An officer of the U.S. Department of Justice responsible for supervising the administration of bankruptcy cases, estates, and trustees; monitoring plans and disclosure statements; monitoring creditors' committees; monitoring fee applications; and performing other statutory duties.

Undersecured claim A debt secured by property that is worth less than the amount of the debt.

Undue hardship The most widely used test for evaluating undue hardship in the dischargeability of a student loan includes three conditions: (1) the debtor cannot maintain—based on current income and expenses—a minimal standard of living if forced to repay the loans; (2) there are indications that the state of affairs is likely to persist for a significant portion of the repayment period; and (3) the debtor made good-faith efforts to repay the loans.

Unlawful detainer action A lawsuit brought by a landlord against a tenant to evict the tenant from rental property—usually for nonpayment of rent.

Unliquidated claim A claim for which a specific value has not been determined.

Unscheduled debt A debt that should have been listed by the debtor in the schedules filed with the court but was not. (Depending on the circumstances, an unscheduled debt may or may not be discharged.)

Unsecured claim A claim or debt for which a creditor holds no special assurance of payment, such as a mortgage or lien; a debt for which credit was extended based solely upon the creditor's assessment of the debtor's future ability to pay.

Uphold The appellate court agrees with the lower court decision and allows it to stand. See affirmed.

V

Venue The geographic area in which a court has jurisdiction. A change of venue is a change or transfer of a case from one judicial district to another.

Verdict The decision of a trial jury or a judge that determines the guilt or innocence of a criminal defendant, or that determines the final outcome of a civil case.

Voir dire French, meaning "say the truth." Jury selection process of questioning prospective jurors, to ascertain their qualifications and determine any basis for challenge.

Voluntary transfer A transfer of a debtor's property with the debtor's consent.

W

Wage garnishment A nonbankruptcy legal proceeding whereby a plaintiff or creditor seeks to subject to his or her claim the future wages of a debtor. In other words, the creditor seeks to have part of the debtor's future wages paid to the creditor for a debt owed to the creditor.

Warrant Court authorization, most often for law enforcement officers, to conduct a search or make an arrest.

Witness A person called upon by either side in a lawsuit to give testimony before the court or jury.

Writ A written court order directing a person to take, or refrain from taking, a certain act.

Writ of certiorari An order issued by the U.S. Supreme Court directing the lower court to transmit records for a case which it will hear on appeal.

Source: *Glossary,* United States Courts, http://www.uscourts.gov/Common/Glossary.aspx (last visited September 12, 2014).

INDEX

B

C

D

E

I

J

K

L

M

N

O

P

R

S

T

U

ABOUT THE AUTHOR

Jasper Kim is a visiting scholar at Stanford University (2014), former visiting scholar at Harvard Law School (2011–12), professor at the Graduate School of International Studies at Ewha Womans University (Seoul, South Korea), and adjunct faculty at the Straus Institute of Dispute Resolution (Pepperdine University School of Law). He will be a Lecturer in Law at the UC Berkeley School of Law (Berkeley Law, 2015). Previously, he worked for Barclays Capital, Credit Suisse, and Lehman Brothers. Jasper Kim is a member of the Washington, D.C. bar and received graduate economic training from the London School of Economics (LSE), graduate legal training from Rutgers University School of Law, and negotiation training at Harvard Law School's Program on Negotiation. He is a contributor to various media, including the BBC, Bloomberg, *The Christian Science Monitor*, CNBC, CNN, *The Los Angeles Times*, NPR, *The New York Times*, Voice of America, and *The Wall Street Journal*. Kim is the founder of the Asia-Pacific Global Research Group (http://www.asiapacificglobal.com).

Jasper Kim's previous books include *ABA Fundamentals: International Economic Systems* (ABA 2012) and *24 Hours with 24 Lawyers: Profiles in Traditional and Non-Traditional Careers* (West 2011).

About the Author